RON HALLIDAY has been investigating paranormal phenomena for twenty years. He is currently chairman of Scottish Earth Mysteries Research, and appears regularly on television and radio, to discuss all aspects of the paranormal. He is a frequent contributer to newspapers and magazines, and is the author of *UFOs: The Scottish Dimension* (1997). Educated at the Universities of Edinburgh and Stirling, Ron is Assistant Registrar at the University of Stirling.

Also by Ron Halliday:

UFOs: THE SCOTTISH DIMENSION

McX

SCOTLAND'S X-FILES

edited and introduced by

RON HALLIDAY

B&W PUBLISHING

First published 1997
by B&W Publishing Ltd
Edinburgh

ISBN 1 873631 77 4

British Library Cataloguing in Publication Data:
A catalogue record for this book is available
from the British Library

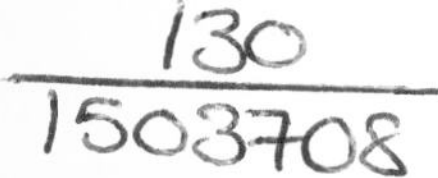

PICTURE CREDITS:

The publishers would like to thank the following
for their invaluable assistance
with the photographs in this book:

Brian Curran, Alec Bell and Margaret Ross for the UFO pictures;
The *Scotsman* Photo Library for the Bob Taylor photos;
Tony Stone Images for the Stealth Aircraft;
Ron Halliday for the Corpach crop circle
and the Fairy Knowe at Aberfoyle;
The Arbroath Herald for the Flannan Isle lighthouse;
Hulton Getty for the Duke of Kent
and Aleister Crowley;
The *Herald* Picture Library for Willie McRae;
Scottish Highland Photo Library for Ben Alder
and the Ring of Brodgar;
Northern Constabulary for the Ben Alder man;
The Still Moving Picture Co. for Callanish,
Boleskine House and Glamis Castle.

Cover Design: Winfortune & Associates

Printed by WSOY

ACKNOWLEDGEMENTS

The publishers would like to thank
the following for their invaluable contribution
to this book. Without them, none of this
would have been possible.

Ron Halliday
James Robertson
Spencer Ashton
Claire Edwards
Ian D. McGellichar
N. D. Goodfield

We would also like to thank
Margaret Ross, Brian Curran and Alec Bell
for permission to use stills from their videos.

EXPLANATORY NOTE

The classifications used
in the file information sections
at the start of each chapter are
fully explained in Appendix A.

The names of certain witnesses
have been changed in order to
preserve their anonymity

CONTENTS

SECTION I
UFOs

SECTION II
UNEXPLAINED

SECTION III
DARK SECRETS

INTRODUCTION

As the tide turns towards more serious investigation of the paranormal, and at a time when public interest in the subject has never been greater, the truth remains elusive. But what exactly is it that we are dealing with when we speak of the paranormal? The list of subjects covered in this book is extensive, highlighting the extraordinary diversity of phenomena currently under investigation—everything from ghosts, poltergeists and UFOs, to nature spirits, crop circles, loch monsters and the occult. Is there really any link between them?

The answer to that is a definite 'yes'. For one thing, mainstream science wholly rejects all of the above topics as being unworthy of investigation, and governments around the world operate a policy of strict secrecy, denying that they have any interest in the paranormal, while at the same time carrying out top-secret research into all manner of strange phenomena. In addition, there have now been so many eyewitness reports of all these phenomena that it is becoming increasingly difficult to dismiss them out of hand.

Any acceptance of UFOs, ghosts or other phenomena does, however, raise major issues for us, and many questions which we cannot, as yet, answer. For example, if there are ghosts does that mean there is life after death? If UFOs are real what does that mean for the Earth's place in the universe? How would we react to learning that we are not alone? And could our ancestors, when space travel was not even a distant dream, use the power of ley-lines to communicate with other worlds and other dimensions? Do unknown lines of energy running underground explain high incidences of mysterious illness clusters which have so far defied scientific explanation? And why is it that some areas of Scotland witness hundreds of UFO sightings, while other areas report only a few.

This book is a wide-ranging investigation of the many and varied manifestations of the paranormal, and the details of strange and unexplained encounters recorded here are not easy to dismiss out of hand. One of the most famous Scottish UFO cases investigated is that of Bob Taylor, who came within yards of a disc-shaped UFO while working near Dechmont Law. This was his one and only strange encounter. He knows what he saw that day and he will never forget it. In common with many other witnesses, Bob had nothing to gain by reporting what happened to him, but he is not prepared to deny it simply because some say 'it cannot have happened'. Similarly, it would be much easier for many of the other witnesses whose experiences are dealt with in this book simply to keep their stories to themselves and not report what they have seen. For these people, however, an overwhelming natural curiosity makes silence impossible. The only way to further our understanding of the paranormal is to encourage people to report their experiences and express their doubts about 'official versions' of events.

The official attitude to the unexplained may, however, be changing. UFO investigation recently became the subject of controversy in the UK Parliament, when the European Union gave the go-ahead to a project to establish an observatory in France for the purpose of monitoring UFOs in the skies over Europe. One Tory MP, Sir Teddy Taylor, commented that 'The whole idea seems to have been cooked up in some ethereal dream-world. . . . I don't know how grown men could be brought to consider such things'. I wrote to Sir Teddy pointing out that, both in Russia and the United States, there was definite government interest in reports of UFOs, and both governments had spent a great deal of money on investigating whether psychic abilities have any military application. In a well-documented case, one former US Army officer, David Moorhouse, has claimed that he and others were involved in top-secret 'psychic warfare' research. This involved so-called 'remote viewing' techniques which were directed against targets in Iraq during the 1990 Gulf War. It has also recently emerged that even our own Ministry of Defence had a section which monitored UFO incidents.

This new European initiative is at an early stage, and

theories of government conspiracies and cover-ups persist. Our government may well know a lot more about UFOs than they are prepared to admit, and, given the resources at their disposal, it would be surprising if they were not well-informed. It could well be that they are as puzzled as everyone else regarding the significance of a particular phenomenon, and what it may represent—yet their attitude towards UFOs has been far from passive, and there remain many unanswered questions over the level of their involvement. To what extent, for example, were the authorities involved in the notorious Cedric Allingham hoax in the 1950s? A hoax which discredited research into UFOs for years.

There are many other, less celebrated, incidents which remain shrouded in mystery and cloaked in theories of cover-up. One such case is that of Willie McRae, who died a lonely, and largely unexplained death beside a quiet country road. A leading Scottish Nationalist, although not a household name, McRae is said to have had many contacts in the shadowy world of the secret intelligence community—links which, it has been argued, were to cost him his life and lead to a bizarre cover-up. And if there was a cover-up in such a seemingly low-profile case, this would lend weight to theories of covert government involvement in other cases—such as the recent spate of UFO sightings in the 'Falkirk Triangle'.

It cannot be denied that there is a long-established climate of secrecy in this country. Those in positions of authority often seem determined to keep the vast majority of the population in ignorance—Willie McRae's alleged suicide and the death of the Duke of Kent are two examples which graphically illustrate Britain's long-standing obsession with secrecy.

A lack of conventional scientific proof leads many people to dismiss all strange phenomena out of hand. Why does the scientific establishment adopt such a negative attitude towards reports of paranormal activity, when numerous scientists have an interest in the unexplained, though they often prefer to keep quiet rather than admit their interest publicly? If a person claims to have seen a UFO, why does their account attract such intense scepticism? Our senses are our window on the world and nobody doubts it when we hear someone say that they have witnessed a traffic or other accident. We may never have seen one ourselves, yet we know that they can happen. We know people to whom these things have happened. Yet the same standards of belief do not seem to apply to reports of paranormal activity. Our society is so used to things it can pigeonhole that anything which does not fit in neatly immediately becomes suspect. In looking at paranormal phenomena, we do not have to suspend our rational faculties, but we must ask whether the view which demands the evidence be fully acceptable by current standards of conventional science is necessarily always the correct one. There has been a century of systematic investigation of ghosts, for example, without conclusive scientific proof having been obtained one way or the other. Perhaps if we are to progress, we must look at the unexplained in a new way—from a different perspective.

Most paranormal investigators readily accept that the majority of UFO cases and many reports of paranormal activity have a straightforward explanation. People regularly misidentify stars and planets as extraterrestrial craft. I once received a video from a witness who had filmed Venus for an hour thinking that a UFO had been hovering close to his house. And, given the right circumstances, almost any odd sound can become the footsteps of a phantom.

But it is the cases which are difficult to explain by any rational means that become the stuff of mystery. And the fact that incidents cannot be explained in accepted ways does not mean that they should be dismissed—as was once the case, it should be remembered, with the existence of dinosaurs and meteorites. It is true that, for example, we have never caught the Loch Ness monster. Therefore, the sceptics would say, it clearly does not exist. In direct opposition to this view is the mass of evidence, from the thousands of eyewitness reports, of a previously unknown aquatic creature which looks very much like a long-extinct dinosaur. Some of these encounters took place when the individuals involved were only feet away from the animal. Eyewitness testimony is eyewitness testimony. Should it be ignored because we do not like or cannot accept the implications of such evidence? Of course, we do not have to be credulous. People exaggerate and fantasise. But taking individual accounts seriously is like listening to someone in the witness box—we have the opportunity to make up our own minds.

Science has advanced a long way in the last hundred

years, and advances will continue into the future. Even so, our understanding of the Earth and of the universe is still so limited that it simply does not make sense to close our eyes to things we cannot yet explain.

Ron Halliday
October 1997

'We live our lives under the twin categories of time and space, and when the two come together we get the great moment.'

John Buchan, *Memory Hold-the-Door*

SECTION I

UFO

UNIDENTIFIED FLYING OBJECTS

FILE NO: 001
SUBJECT: ......Close Encounter/attempted abduction
LOCATION: ....Dechmont Law, nr. Livingston
DATE: ....November 1979
CLASSIFICATION: .... CEII
STATUS: .... open

THE LIVINGSTON ENCOUNTER

November 9th 1979 dawned cold and clear. The 3 a.m. edition of *The Scotsman* newspaper led on the furore over an 'IRA Stunt'. Jim Callaghan, the Prime Minister, had condemned the BBC for allegedly filming an IRA propaganda exercise in Northern Ireland.

On an inside page, Albert Morris's column was entitled: 'Reflections of an Alien Kind'. In the article he discussed the attitude of extraterrestrials to an encounter with Earthlings and wrote, 'It is not space monsters we have to fear . . . but mankind itself'. It was almost as if he had foreseen the astonishing event that was to take place that very morning.

The object that was to cause such controversy may well have made its first appearance at 8.05 a.m. A driver, Graham Kennedy, heading west on the A89, was passing Bangour

Hospital when he noticed a bright light above and to the left of his car. It accelerated towards him a few feet above the ground, on a collision course. Swerving to avoid a crash with the orange-coloured, torch-shaped object, he nearly rammed a car heading in the opposite direction. Fortunately, both cars managed to stop before impact, but the driver of the second vehicle claimed that he had seen nothing of the mysterious light which had come so close to causing a serious crash. Both men might be forgiven for believing that the unidentified object was a figment of the imagination of someone who, as the day was just beginning, was not quite fully awake.

Curiously, a remarkably similar event occurred near Warminster in England in 1965—an area which, after dozens of UFO sightings, became known as the 'UFO Capital of the Western World'. On 10th August 1965 Terry Pell was driving his lorry to Warminster when a ball of flaming crimson light sped across the sky, then floated down towards his cab in a head-on motion, threatening to smash through the windscreen. Mr Pell, like Mr Kennedy a decade later, swerved to avoid an impact and slid off the road. There were no other witnesses as his wife and daughter, though in the cab with him, slept through the entire incident. Luckily, however, there were other witnesses to the Bangour sighting that morning in 1979. A van driver, also heading west on the A89, towards the town of Broxburn, saw a bright light in the sky. Though stationary, it struck him as too big to be a star or a planet. The light flashed intermittently on and off, and then gradually grew dimmer. Eventually, as nothing else of significance occurred, the driver moved on, but the memory of the strange event remained firmly fixed in his mind.

Around the same time, a young nurse, Anne MacGregor, stepped from her bus and started to walk along the A89 towards Bangour hospital. As she went, Anne heard a distant but distinct hissing noise. Glancing upwards, she caught sight of a bright yellow light that appeared to be descending above the area known as Deans, near to a hill called Dechmont Law on the fringe of the New Town of Livingston.

A few minutes later, a cyclist travelling to work at a tyre factory in nearby Newbridge village, stopped at a junction before making a right turn. As he did so, he spotted a bright yellowish light that appeared to be hovering over the M8 motorway, close to Deer Hill—the local name for Dechmont Law.

Did the object land on Deer Hill? If it did, there are no known witnesses to the touchdown, and for the following three hours no more mysterious lights were reported. But then an incident occurred, the implications of which were to reverberate around the world wherever UFOs are discussed.

Robert Taylor was well-respected as an honest, dedicated forestry worker. A few years off retirement age at 61, Bob was employed by Livingston Development Corporation working in the woodland areas in the vicinity of the New Town. At around 11 a.m. on 9th November Bob, in the company of his dog Lara, a seven-year-old red setter, was making his way through the covering of fir trees lying on the lower slopes of Dechmont Law. As he approached a clearing in the wood he was shocked to see twelve yards in front of him a large, circular object. According to some accounts it was supported by three metal legs, although Bob himself has not verified this. The object was dark metallic grey, and around the circumference Bob noted a distinct narrow flange. It did not move, and in places it seemed transparent, which contrasted sharply with other surfaces which looked like giant sections of emery paper.

As Bob cautiously approached the mystery object, two small spherical devices, similar to World War Two naval mines with spikes protruding all round, suddenly dropped to the ground. It appeared to Bob that they had come from inside the 'craft' and he caught a whiff of a strong, pungent smell which brought on a choking sensation. Over the noise of his dog furiously barking, Bob heard a clear hissing sound (as nurse Anne MacGregor had earlier). The next thing he remembered is coming to, his face pressed hard against the wet ground.

His legs were aching, but through the pain he managed to note that the two spheres and the 'mother' object had disappeared. The barking in his ears confirmed that the faithful Lara had not abandoned him, but Bob was for the moment unable to calm the dog's fear, as he had lost the ability to speak.

In a state of shock, Bob struggled to his feet, but he was unable to get his lorry started, and so he staggered the mile back to his home in Livingston. It was later suggested that it was during this confused period that Bob ripped his trousers, as he scrambled over a barbed-wire fence. The straight, neat lines made by the tears, however, would seem to contradict this.

Bob's wife Mary was deeply shocked when she saw the state her husband was in, and didn't know what to think when he told her he had been attacked by a spaceship, assuring him 'there's no such thing'. Acting quickly, she phoned the doctor, then Bob's boss, Malcolm Drummond, Head of the Forestry Department, to report the incident. A quick check round Dechmont Law by other forestry workers failed to reveal anything out of the ordinary. No sign of an alien craft. Nor of a band of marauding thugs, an explanation which had automatically suggested itself to some who heard of the incident.

The local police had been alerted and, from their Livingston base, soon arrived at the scene of the 'crime'. Bob joined the officers, headed by Detective Inspector Ian Wark, having insisted on revisiting the spot where he had been attacked. The police and victim noted extensive ladder-shaped impressions in the ground just where Bob thought the 'craft' had been standing. Indentations revealed the path along which, Bob explained, the spherical objects approached him. Marks in the earth lent support to Bob's belief that he had been dragged towards the larger object before being released.

The police took Bob's account very seriously and a criminal investigation was soon under way. In spite of the extensive publicity, however, and a widespread search, no clue as to the source of Bob's attack was ever unearthed. The file on his encounter remains open to this day.

The police did confirm in their enquiries that Bob's trousers bore two significant tears which had been made in an upward direction. His legs were cut and bruised in the same area. Someone or something had clearly caught hold of Bob in a grip powerful enough to leave tell-tale marks.

Interest in the incident, now one of the most famous in the annals of ufology, has remained high. Bob Taylor has consistently stood by his account, and the character of the man (his boss called him 'sensible and straightforward') has convinced many that an encounter of great significance occurred that day on windswept Dechmont Law.

Understandably, given the closeness of the encounter, those who deny the existence of UFOs have attempted to put forward a variety of explanations. Scottish sceptic Steuart Campbell has suggested various possibilities, including ball lightning, a mirage of Venus or Bob's having suffered an epileptic fit. Mr Campbell's solutions have, however, met with little support.

In 1992 Scottish ufologist Ken Higgins, and Ron Halliday of the Scottish Earth Mysteries Research group, with the co-operation of Livingston Development Corporation, were instrumental in having a plaque erected to mark the site of this historic incident—the first time that a UFO site has been officially recognised. Sadly, the original plaque was stolen, but plans are being made by SEMR to have a more solid and fitting monument put in its place.

Significantly, witness accounts of incidents which took place around this time continue to emerge. In October 1992 Mr A. Ferguson of Edinburgh reported that while parking his lorry in a lay-by at around 8 p.m. on 8th November 1979 he noticed a strip of brilliant light, shaped like a ruler, heading for Dechmont Law. Another witness, Mrs E. Scott, claimed that while she stood at a bus stop looking towards the Pentland Hills she saw a round silvery object with flashing lights. At first she thought it must be a helicopter. She realised it was nothing of the sort and 'must be a UFO' when the object shot off at high speed towards Dechmont Law and disappeared. Mrs Scott, understandably, is uncertain of the exact date of this incident. She is sure, however, that it happened either on the day of Bob's encounter or the previous evening. Whatever the day, it is clear that Dechmont was a hot-bed of strange events around this time.

The Dechmont Law sighting has come to be seen as a key incident in the development of Scottish ufology. It put Scotland on the world UFO map, while at the same time inspiring various individuals to enter the neglected area of UFO investigation.

FILE NO: 002
SUBJECT: .... UFO hot-spot
LOCATION: .... area around Falkirk
DATE: ....1992 to present
CLASSIFICATION: ....CEI, MA1
STATUS: ....under investigation

THE FALKIRK TRIANGLE

Situated within the so-called 'Falkirk Triangle', Bonnybridge has been labelled the 'UFO capital of Scotland', and is now widely regarded to be a UFO 'hot-spot'. The surrounding area has also witnessed intense UFO activity, with numerous sightings reported from Stirling in the west to Fife and the fringes of Edinburgh in the east, while West Lothian has experienced a frequency of incidents out of all proportion to its size and population density.

If, as local councillor Billy Buchanan has claimed, Bonnybridge (population 5,500) does indeed have over 2,000 witnesses to UFO sightings then it truly is a world hot-spot. A similar proportion of witnesses to population in Edinburgh would mean around 200,000 people had seen a UFO in Scotland's capital.

The recent spate of sightings in the area started quietly enough with a number of interesting although typical UFO reports. These incidents began in January 1992 when Mr James Walker witnessed a cross-shaped formation of stars hovering above the road as he was driving along. He stopped his car and looked back, noting that the lights had now assumed a triangular shape. Mr Walker was understandably mystified by the incident which he felt could not be put down to any obvious source, such as an aircraft.

Perhaps the best known incident took place in March of that year. At around 7 p.m. the Slogett family were walking towards Bonnybridge when Steven Slogett caught sight of a circle of light. He drew the attention of the rest of the family to the strange light, before it appeared to land in a nearby field. As the family walked on, they were halted in their tracks by a football-sized blue light hovering above the road ahead. Isabella Slogett later reported, 'My daughter Carole and I saw a UFO land right in front of us. A door opened and there was a howling sound. I screamed and ran off terrified'. According to Carole, 'There was a flash of light as if we were being photographed'. When they reached their home in Bonnybridge, the mysterious object was still visible and was seen by several other witnesses.

Reports continued throughout 1992. In November, for example, a Mr Anderson reporting a 'bluish white light, very bright, which disappeared behind clouds', and a father and daughter witnessed an unidentified triangular-shaped object.

Another interesting report occurred in 1993 when Ray and Cathy Proceck, driving to Cumbernauld to visit friends, spotted 'an elliptical shape with bright lights around the edge'. As they passed beneath a viaduct they opened the sunroof of their car to get a better look. When they reached the other side they saw 'an identical craft'. Both objects were triangular-shaped and completely silent. Before the incident neither Ray nor Cathy were interested in UFOs, but both were convinced that they had seen something they could not explain.

It was not the nature of the incidents, however, which attracted media interest in the area, but rather the sheer volume of sightings which were relayed to the media by local councillor, Billy Buchanan. He explained that his constituents were coming forward with reports of UFO encounters and that it was his duty, therefore, to seek an explanation of the incidents.

By the end of December 1992 over 200 witnesses to unexplained events were being cited by Councillor Buchanan and a public 'skywatch' was announced on TV. As a result, a considerable amount of publicity was generated, although to the disappointment of those who turned up, including the TV cameras, no UFO activity was observed. All this publicity simply led to even more reports of UFO sightings and some ufologists began to question whether it was now possible to disentangle the original reports from the many new sightings inevitably created by media interest. It is well known that individual reports of UFO incidents increase after existing incidents are highlighted: what previously was simply a light in the sky becomes a UFO.

In order to calm the situation, a public meeting was arranged at the Norwood Hotel in Bonnybridge by Billy Buchanan for Sunday 31st January 1993 at 7 p.m. The *Sunday Post* newspaper reported that, 'A town plagued by UFOs has called in the experts as concern grows among residents'. Councillor Buchanan was amongst those claiming to have seen a UFO and added, 'I've had around 400 calls in the past few months'. The article revealed that some of the town's residents were to be 'hypnotised in a bid to find any subconscious memories of being taken aboard an alien spacecraft'. In the event the hypnotist did not turn up—although an audience of almost 300 did, to hear Malcolm Robinson lecture on worldwide UFO incidents, including alleged abduction cases.

At this point Scottish Earth Mysteries Research, in a radio broadcast, urged caution over the Bonnybridge sightings until a proper investigation had been carried out and the number and nature of the sightings could be accurately assessed. As events moved rapidly along, however, it was clear that media interest was not going to subside.

The arrival of a Japanese film crew provided the opportunity for some interesting speculation on the Bonnybridge sightings. In the *Stirling Observer* Malcolm Robinson was quoted as being convinced that Bonnybridge is one of the world's few 'windows' to another dimension. Meanwhile, according to the reporter, Councillor Buchanan had more than UFOs on his mind—the suggestion being that it had been his intention from the start to generate favourable publicity for Bonnybridge. But, as Councillor Buchanan was reported to have said, 'Why shouldn't Bonnybridge benefit? We have a superb setting here and Central Region is a friendly and inviting place'. The article concluded with the revelation that 'Councillor Buchanan has a special surprise in store for the Japanese group—a massive cake shaped like a flying saucer'. The Japanese were suitably impressed by this display of Bonnybridgean hospitality. However, attempts to secure financial backing for a 'giant glass mushroom-shaped visitor centre', intended as a UFO tourist attraction, failed to get off the ground, according to *The Daily Record*.

Meanwhile, as Bonnybridge was staking its claim to be a 'world hot-spot' for UFOs, the same description was also being applied to Edinburgh, a mere twenty miles to the east. The question was being asked: were the UFOs seen in Bonnybridge identical to those appearing over the Lothians? Disappointingly, as Scottish ufologists argued about the nature of the Bonnybridge sightings, the opportunity for a comparison—piecing together the central belt UFO jigsaw—was overlooked.

Meetings arranged in Falkirk, whilst attracting huge attention and raising the profile of ufology in Scotland, did not really move the investigation forward and, by encouraging people to consider every odd light in the sky a 'UFO', may have muddied the waters rather than cleared them.

Some aspects of the Bonnybridge experience degenerated

into farce, as writer Edward Talisman noted in *Phenomenal News*. Describing the controversy over a supposed alien called 'Zal-us', Mr Talisman wrote:

> Sceptics of the Bonnybridge "hot-spot" were given added fuel by the unfortunate antics involving "Zal-us" and the "Council of Nine". Zal-us, according to some newspaper reports, was an alien who had an important message to give to the world. The message was going to be revealed at a meeting in Falkirk Town Hall, one evening in October. The hall had been booked for the affair, by Councillor Billy Buchanan, no less.
>
> So Councillor Billy was at the centre of this enigma? The tabloids seemed to think so and one (the *Daily Star*, I think) labelled the unfortunate Buchanan "Bonnybridge's Crackpot Councillor". Indeed, to be fair to the press, someone, somewhere, seemed to have put words into Billy's mouth which appear to suggest that he had personally met an ET who claimed membership of some galactic body which was overseeing the development of the Earth (obvious, isn't it?).
>
> All in all, it made a great read, and, caught up in the excitement, I was devastated to learn that it had all been a load of . . . nonsense. Billy Buchanan had never met an alien, and the name Zal-us was alien (all right, completely unknown) to him. Mr Buchanan was, it transpires, utterly blameless, and bemused and justifiably annoyed at his name being taken in vain.
>
> So where did "Zal-us" come from? Without revealing all the twists and turns of a murky plot, it seems that another UFO group had somehow picked up the name. But where from, I don't know. Anyway, according to *The Scotsman* the name originated with ufologist Malcolm Robinson in his newsletter. However, claims Malcolm: "I don't know how the name

> Zal-us crept into the article . . . I would never put in some false data . . . just to jazz it up!" An enigma indeed!

While all this was going on, genuinely odd incidents were taking place in the area. In October 1994 three cleaners, while on their way to work at the Union Chemical Factory at Carronshire, saw five UFOs. Beatrice Campbell reported that she had first noticed the UFOs at around 5.40 a.m. She described one large object which had an orange glow and four smaller ones sparkling on and off. The larger object appeared to be sending out beams of light to the smaller sparkling objects. Beatrice reported the sighting to her manager, Bill Downie. Soon other employees were coming forward to give their accounts, which seemed to indicate that strange objects had been appearing in the area for some days. The previous Wednesday at 7 p.m., Diane Keating from Camelon had witnessed a reddish-coloured ball which disappeared and then reappeared. She was sure it could not have been an aircraft because she saw one fly under it. At the same time Steve Lewisham saw a 'bright white' object which moved away from them, then 'came back and began to glow red and orange. It was going really fast. We saw a passenger plane with its landing lights on underneath it. The object was very much faster than the plane.'

One fascinating aspect of the UFO sightings in this area is the frequency with which UFOs have been caught on video. According to the *Falkirk Herald* one was even captured on police video cameras, which filmed an object reported by

Catherine Penman of Hallglen, near Falkirk. Her husband, Scott Penman, first spotted the UFO at around 10 p.m. According to Catherine, 'It was a really bright light which was down quite low. At first, I thought it was a star, but it was ten times bigger than a star and was really close to the house. There is no way it could have been a helicopter or a plane because of the length of time it hovered in the air. I contacted the police because it was so unusual.'

Even greater publicity was given to video footage taken by sixty-three-year-old Margaret Ross of Stenhousemuir. Her video of an object seen in May 1996 shows a bright light criss-crossed by stripes of different colours. Margaret and her husband Alex spotted the UFO as they were preparing for bed, and it appeared to them to be disc-shaped and brighter than a star. As they videoed it, the UFO appeared to zoom toward the house. There is certainly no doubting the unsettling nature of the couple's experience, although some UFO investigators believe that the camera may have unintentionally doctored the image of a natural object.

However, in October of the same year Margaret Ross caught another UFO on video. At first the white object which she was videoing to the south of her house pulsated for about 15 minutes. Then it gradually changed, transforming into a half moon shape with intensely bright diagonal bars and a glowing outer shell. Mrs Ross noticed the UFO after she got out of bed at around 6 a.m. By a strange coincidence, her daughter Alison had also spotted the same object from her front room window a couple of miles away. She watched it for some time before ringing her mother at 7 a.m. to draw it to her attention. Mrs Ross, who had by then already been videoing the UFO for an hour, was delighted to have independent confirmation of what she had seen

More remarkable video footage was taken in October 1996, this time by Hallglen resident Barry Macdonald. Barry was driving along Windsor Road in the Camelon district of Falkirk when he and his girlfriend Jane Adamson spotted a mysterious object hovering in the sky. It was around 6.40 p.m. when they stopped the car and got out to take a closer look. After they had watched the object for several minutes, Barry remembered that he had his video camera on the back seat. Barry is a keen angler and to prove the size of his catch he makes sure he has the evidence on tape. This time he was going to use his camera to even greater effect. Although he only managed to film the object for about 30 seconds before it disappeared, his footage was to cause a worldwide sensation, and appear on TV programmes across five continents. The UFO on his tape is an orange oval which seems to change shape, becoming a white disc—the classic 'flying saucer' shape. It seems to glow orange again, then turn white once more before disappearing. Whether it simply 'vanishes' or moves away at an incredibly high speed is impossible to tell—it is there one moment and gone the next. Checks with local airports indicated that no aircraft were in the vicinity at the time.

In November 1995, Brian Curran's home near Polbeth, Bathgate, was 'buzzed by a fireball UFO', according to *The*

Sun newspaper. The report also claimed that 'the huge blazing craft appeared just yards from them as they cleared up after a party'. Although, in fact, the orange object remained some distance away in the night sky, the video footage was clearly shows that something very strange took place. The UFO appeared as a bright orange disc and had the characteristics of a three-dimensional object. Its surface was ruffled—one commentator described it as like a baby's rusk. The most intriguing aspects of the mystery object were the two semicircular gaps, one at the bottom and the second on the lower right, which in the early frames look like monstrous bites out of a round cheese. It is as if a mechanism is in operation, and two smooth coated sections move out of the main body to fill the empty spaces. As Brian and his wife Shirley continued watching, the object disappeared, then reappeared, then shot off again at an amazing rate and vanished. Air Traffic Control at Edinburgh Airport reported that there had been no unusual sightings that night.

Interestingly, in February 1996 a similar object was filmed over Inverness, and days before the Curran encounter an almost identical UFO was filmed over Norwich in England. In November 1996 Alec Bell of Fauldhouse in West Lothian captured a UFO on video which bore a striking resemblance to the one seen on the Curran video. Mr Bell observed the UFO for 30-40 minutes and his footage clearly shows a glowing disc-shaped object in the sky. Just as in Brian Curran's video, sections are missing from its rim.

Analysis of Brian Curran's video was undertaken by John

Morrison, who, after an extensive examination, confirmed that an unidentified object had definitely been filmed, although he was of the opinion that it was in fact arrow-shaped rather than oval. What it actually was, however, remains unexplained.

If Nick Pope, the Ministry of Defence executive officer turned ufologist, is correct, there have been over 8,000 witnesses to UFO sightings in this area—a truly staggering figure. Councillor Billy Buchanan, who played such a key role in focusing the attention of UFO experts on the events in his town, claimed a figure of 2,000 witnesses. It may be that Mr Pope, with his insider's knowledge of official UFO monitoring, was aware of a larger group of reports which have not yet reached the public domain. It is very much to be hoped that in the not-too-distant future the full extent of UFO sightings in the 'Falkirk Triangle' area will be revealed and fresh light thrown on a genuine Scottish mystery.

FILE NO: 003
SUBJECT: .... Close Encounter/alien abduction
LOCATION: .... A70, nr. Balerno
DATE: .... August 1992
CLASSIFICATION: .... CEIV
STATUS: .... open

'IN A VOID OF BLACKNESS . . .'

One case, which has received a great deal of media attention, is largely based on testimony which emerged when the two witnesses later underwent hypnotic regression.

On the 17th August 1992 Gary Wood and Colin Wright had a close encounter of a very strange kind. The two men were delivering a satellite TV system to a friend in the village of Tarbrax, 15 miles outside the city of Edinburgh. They set off at around 10 p.m., expecting the journey to take no more than half an hour. But it was to take them well over two hours to reach their destination.

The A70, once it passes through the outlying suburbs of Currie and Balerno, almost immediately enters a bleak expanse of moor that stretches the length of the Pentland Hills all the way to Carnwath. This desolate and often inhospitable road is known as the Lang Whang. Tarbrax lies off the main road and is itself an extremely isolated place.

As they drove towards Harperrig Reservoir, about five miles from Balerno, the car was approaching a blind bend in the road when Wood heard Wright call out, 'What the hell is that?' Looking up, he saw a very large object that seemed to be hovering 20 feet above the road. By his reckoning the object was about 30 feet wide, black in colour, and resembled the classic 'flying saucer' shape familiar to him from science-fiction films. Windowless, it looked as if it were made of a solid metallic substance.

Terrified, Wood put his foot down on the accelerator in an attempt to drive underneath the object and get away from the scene as fast as possible. As the car passed under it, they were plunged into what Wood later described as 'a void of blackness'. He also described a 'shimmering curtain' falling around them, rather like the picture on an untuned TV set. In the darkness they felt a shunt on the back of the car and then, what seemed like only moments later, they were back on the starlit road once again.

Wood immediately drove off at high speed, arriving at Tarbrax at 12.45 a.m. He had found the experience deeply disturbing, and his only concern had been to get away as quickly as possible. Both men were amazed to learn that they had arrived about two hours later than expected. They had set off at 10 p.m. It was now 12.45 a.m. the following morning. Their 30-minute journey had taken, inexplicably, five times as long.

After the encounter, Gary began to experience various unpleasant symptoms, including headaches and bouts of extreme nervousness. He quickly connected these sensations with his strange vision on the A70. Having tried, but failed, to contact Scottish Earth Mysteries Research (which had changed address), Gary eventually contacted UFO investigator Malcolm Robinson. Soon afterwards, the two witnesses decided to undergo hypnosis in an attempt to account for the 'missing time' on their journey. It was a brave decision, as BUFORA, Britain's leading UFO research group, had long since abandoned the practice because of the unreliability of the testimony produced.

Following sessions with experienced hypnotherapist Helen Walters, details of an abduction by small grey extraterrestrials emerged. In his account of what took place on board the alien craft, Gary described one of the 'greys' as having 'a translucent bone-shaped arm with long fingers'. He also saw a hole in the floor filled with some kind of thick, sticky fluid. As he looked, he saw 'a head appear out of it with a body and two arms. The creature must have been pretty big, bigger than me. It was like a skeleton with flesh around it. It had long arms, really long arms. It had a long body, really skinny, with the skin tight to the bone'.

He described the entity as having a large head with two prominent, but non-human dark eyes. Its flesh appeared discoloured. These strange beings communicated with Gary using telepathy. Their purpose in abducting him appeared to be to carry out some form of examination. These remembered incidents were far from reassuring for either abductee, although Colin Wright seemed less concerned about the incident than his friend Gary.

The crucial issue in all such cases is whether the details of the abduction incident would have emerged without the patient being hypnotically regressed. Can we be absolutely sure that the account that emerged was genuine, or was it simply the product of a subconscious reworking of a thousand images collected from television, films, books and magazines? It is a long-established fact that hypnosis can lead to witnesses recounting details that are manifestly incorrect. So how do we separate fact from fiction? False-memory syndrome may not be a complete explanation of the A70 case, but it has to be considered as a possibility.

Both witnesses remain adamant about the reality of their encounter, the strange craft they came across and the time missing out of their lives. The delay in reporting it, however, meant that certain vital evidence was not examined. What, for example, happened to Gary's car during the period of the abduction? If they were taken from the car and returned to it at least an hour later, then that vehicle must have been stored or kept somewhere. We will never know what happened to the car during this time, as it was sold on soon after the incident and no testing or inspection was carried out—a real loss to ufology.

Nevertheless, we can be absolutely sure about one thing: something very strange happened that night on the road to Tarbrax. Exactly what it was remains to be determined.

FILE NO: 004
SUBJECT: .... the Lossiemouth UFO
LOCATION: ....Lossiemouth, Moray Coast
DATE: .... February 1954
CLASSIFICATION: .... CEIV
STATUS: .... closed

THE MAN FROM ANOTHER PLANET

In 1956 a young Fleet Air Arm officer took off from *HMS Fulmar*, accompanied by two other aircraft. This was a routine training flight for sub-lieutenant Coates, and the weather was excellent. His mission that day was to film the coastline around Lossiemouth, and when they reached their destination the aircraft were flying at around 15,000 feet. The sky remained clear and empty apart from the three Sea-Hawks. The mission was uneventful and the aircraft returned to base when their task had been completed.

It was only later, when the film was developed, that Lt. Coates realised he had inadvertently filmed a classic example of a 'flying saucer', below the port side of his Sea-Hawk. Lt. Coates was certain that he would have spotted anything flying beneath them as he spent almost the entire time looking through the viewfinder and adjusting the focus of his camera during the mission, so he was astonished at the discovery of the image of the UFO and could not account for it. Nor could the Admiralty when they officially investigated the incident.

An easily-overlooked event in itself, but in view of the extraordinary encounter which was reported to have taken place in the same area only two years previously, Lt. Coates' experience takes on a whole new significance.

On 18th February 1954, Cedric Allingham, an English ornithologist, crossed the border into Scotland, heading for the north coast on a caravanning holiday. He was alone, and had taken the time off to recuperate from ill health. He intended to go to Wick, but in the event he only got as far as Lossiemouth. There he would spend a week, and then, because of what happened to him, he would drive straight back to London and begin to write up his account.

Allingham was 32, of average height, but quite thin. A photograph of him shows a man in a sharp suit and bow-tie, wearing black-rimmed glasses and sporting a moustache, with his hair combed back in typical 1950s style. An unremarkable figure, but what happened to him as he strolled along the coast one afternoon, between Lossiemouth and Buckie, was the most remarkable thing that had ever happened to him, and possibly to anyone else in the world.

As he walked, on the look-out for birdlife, he heard the sound of an engine and what seemed like a swishing noise overhead. The sky was clear except for some cloud to the north. High up above him he could see a dark speck. He got out his binoculars. What he saw was no swooping bird or aeroplane, but something that had the classic shape of a UFO, or, in the more popular terminology of the day, a flying saucer. Allingham could see the sunlight glinting on it—it appeared to be made of metal—and estimated that it was about 5,000 feet up, about the size of a bomber, and tilted at an angle to show an upper dome and spherical landing gear.

The object began to move rapidly north, and upwards. He dropped his binoculars and got out his camera. The three photographs he managed to take captured something on film, but nothing identifiable. They show only a speck in the far distance. Meanwhile the saucer disappeared into the cloud out to sea.

Allingham sat down and ate a sandwich, musing on what he had seen. Perhaps he was mistaken? After a while he continued on his way, but at about 3 p.m. he saw the saucer again, this time at about 10,000 feet. A little later he decided to turn back and retrace his steps to Lossiemouth. Shortly before 4 p.m., the saucer appeared again, this time heading in towards him from the sea.

'There was no doubt,' Allingham wrote later, 'of its intention to land. When it was within a few hundred yards of me, I distinctly heard a low humming sound which I imagine could only have come from the engines. . . . I was too rooted to the spot to do anything for a moment; then I whipped out my camera and took a couple of shots in quick succession, as the saucer was making its final descent. It was heading almost directly towards me. The whole metallic body seemed to glow faintly, and the saucer hovered for a second or two before landing with a soft but audible thud.'

Now Allingham was not unfamiliar with some of the recent literature on space and the possibility of life elsewhere in the universe. Only the year before George Adamski had published *Flying Saucers Have Landed*, a sensational account of a spaceship landing at Palomar in California. Adamski had, it seemed, been selected by the visitors from Venus, and had managed to exchange a certain amount of information with them. There had been a huge amount of public interest, and indeed there had been a spate of sightings, most of them obvious hoaxes, in the following months. Allingham found himself on a deserted stretch of the coast, the sole witness to what appeared to be another visit to Earth by travellers from another planet. At least, he thought, he would have some photographs to prove what he had seen.

The saucer, as he later described it, was about 50 feet in diameter, 20 feet high, and the hull, central wall and dome seemed to be shaped from one sheet of metal. 'There were two visible groups of portholes set in threes round the central wall, above which was a small flange. From the top of the dome a dark vertical rod projected which reminded me of a lightning conductor. I could not guess its function. The spherical landing gear—at three points just inside the base of the hull—looked as if made of some slightly resilient material similar in texture to rubber.'

Allingham moved a little closer. 'As I neared the Saucer, a

sliding panel in the lower part moved back and a man leaped lightly and gracefully to the ground. As he advanced to meet me, I raised my arm in salute. He did the same. And then, for a while, we stood staring at each other.'

The 'spaceman' was humanoid, about 6 feet tall, his skin a curious deep-tan colour, and apart from this and a very high forehead Allingham said that they looked quite alike. He wore a one-piece suit from neck to feet. Only his head and hands were exposed, and some tubes leading from his nose seemed to be some kind of breathing apparatus. According to Allingham, in terrestrial clothes, 'he could have had no difficulty in passing for an Englishman.'

Allingham of course wanted to question where the ship had come from. On a piece of paper he drew a rough diagram of the solar system, with the sun and its nearest three orbiting planets, Mercury, Venus and Earth. Allingham showed this picture to the spaceman, indicating Earth and gesturing that this was where he was from. He then pointed at the circle representing Venus. The spaceman, amazingly, shook his head. Allingham pointed again and said 'Venus'. The spaceman, in a voice that had a liquid quality to it—'the clear liquid of a hillside spring'—repeated the word.

Allingham drew a fourth circle to represent the orbit of Mars. This time, when he pointed at it and said the name 'Mars', the spaceman nodded vigorously.

There was a limit as to how much could be communicated in this way. Remembering part of the Adamski story, Allingham tried to get his messages across telepathically, mentally asking, 'Why have you come here?' But this didn't work. Feeling helpless, he had an overwhelming desire to laugh. 'I pointed to my lips, then to my brain, shook my head and laughed.

'The Martian looked at me and then he, too, laughed. It must have been a ludicrous spectacle—men from different planets standing helplessly on a lonely part of the Scottish coast, laughing at each other's efforts to make one another understand.'

To show his friendliness, Allingham made the Martian a gift of his red fountain-pen. This was accepted and put in a pocket of the Martian's suit, but nothing was given in exchange.

Returning to his pictures, Allingham drew a larger picture of Mars, marking on it the so-called 'canals'. The Martian seemed to recognise. After much to-ing and fro-ing, Allingham was able to establish that the canals did indeed hold water. They had been built to store the precious resource when the planet began to dry up long before, but since then the Martians had learnt how to manufacture water, which they still kept in the canals, using them to irrigate the nearby land. Allingham also established that the Martians had been in contact with the Venusians. Their visits to Earth were increasing because they were extremely worried about Earthmen's intentions of exploring space. They feared the export of war, especially in the form of nuclear weapons. Both Martians and Venusians wanted to help humans to learn to live at peace with one another.

It was time to go. The Martian would not allow Allingham into his craft, but as he walked back to it alone, Allingham took a photograph of him retreating into the spaceship. The saucer took off and headed out to sea. Allingham looked at his watch. It was 4.25 p.m. His interview had lasted nearly half an hour.

But who would believe him? The story seemed too extraordinary, and he had no witnesses. Then, as he walked back to his caravan, he met a man whom he had seen earlier in the day. This was a fisherman called James Duncan, who had been coming down a hill and had seen the last few minutes of the encounter. Allingham persuaded him to write out and sign a statement swearing to the truth of what he had seen.

Later that year, Allingham's account was published as a book, *Flying Saucer From Mars*. It was sensational. Thousands of copies were sold. There were, however, many sceptics. It seemed incriminating that Allingham should have had such an experience only a year after the publication of Adamski's hugely successful book. Was it only to be expected that the very murky photographs in Allingham's book, showing what looked like a large hubcap but without any background visible to show perspective, were of an object so similar to the saucers seen by Adamski? As for the picture of the Martian, Robert Chapman, the science correspondent of the *Sunday Express*, wrote that it 'showed the hazy back-view of someone in the middle distance walking away from the camera, who admittedly *might* be a man from Mars but could equally well have been a man from Margate.' To the modern eye, the tall man looks like a rather distorted version of George Orwell disappearing into a fog. Was there deliberate irony in Allingham's remark that his spaceman could have passed for an Englishman? In short, was he taking a gullible public for a ride?

Chapman and others tried to contact Allingham through his publisher, Frederick Muller Limited. But, contrary to the usual marketing practices of publishers, the author was not available for interview. He had been ill—that, after all, had been the reason for his holiday in the first place—and was, it was implied, suffering from tuberculosis. His condition had worsened and he had gone to Switzerland to recover. Soon, it was being reported that Cedric Allingham was dead.

The reporters could find no evidence, other than his book, that such a man had ever existed. Nor, when inquiries were made, could anybody by the name of James Duncan be found to confirm his own written testimony. The picture of Allingham, looked at again, became suspicious in itself. The bow-tie, the glasses, the moustache—were these perhaps elements of a disguise? In later years, some researchers would even suggest that a hoax had been pulled by none other than the astronomer Patrick Moore, in an effort to show how ludicrous some of the UFO stories circulating could be. Moore has himself neither confirmed nor denied this story. Certainly, the stereotypical descriptions now seem utterly ridiculous. Would a Martian nod and shake his head to indicate yes and no? Would he speak back in the way described? Scientific developments have since proved that no humanoid life, indeed life of any sort, exists on Mars, and that there is no water on the planet. Earth technology has landed on Mars and the most exciting things found so far are some new kinds of rocks.

In retrospect, the most touching aspect of this case was the Martian's concern about the nuclear arms race. The mid-1950s saw the Cold War in full swing: could Cedric Allingham, or whoever was behind him, have wanted to get a serious message across with maximum publicity, by having it delivered by an extraterrestrial being?

'I am certain in my own mind,' wrote Robert Chapman in his own book, *UFO: Flying Saucers Over Britain?*, published in 1969, 'that Cedric Allingham, if an author of that name ever really existed, did *not* have the experience he claimed—or anything like it. As for his "death" in Switzerland, I suggest this was no more than a device to put an end to inquiries for him.

'In my view, there is a strong likelihood that "Cedric Allingham" is still alive, in excellent health and far from repentant at having pulled a fast one on thousands of credulous saucerers.'

As for Mr Allingham, perhaps the last word on this matter should be with him:

'When someone decides one day that the time has come to write the history of interplanetary communication from its beginnings,' Allingham wrote in his book, 'George Adamski will no doubt have an important place in it. Cedric Allingham will not! I have no illusions about myself; I am certain that my encounter with the Martian Saucer . . . was due to nothing more than chance. At best I shall be remembered as an amateur scientist who had the good fortune to be the first Briton who met a man from another planet. And that is how I should like it to be.'

FILE NO: 005
SUBJECT: ....Close Encounter/MIBs
LOCATION: .... Blairgowrie, Perthshire
DATE: .... April 1984
CLASSIFICATION: .... CEI, AN5
STATUS: .... open

THE BLAIRGOWRIE INCIDENT

The Perthshire region of Scotland, better known for its tourist attractions, has recently witnessed a series of bizarre UFO incidents. The focus of this activity is the village of Blairgowrie situated on the banks of the River Ericht. During the summer months, visitors arrive from all parts of Britain, unaware of the strange events that have periodically shattered the quiet harmony of the countryside and the lives of the local people.

Take Sid Freeman. Sid is a talented craftsman and restorer of antique furniture. Nothing he had ever experienced could have prepared him for the strange encounter that took place at his home in Blairgowrie on April 25th 1984.

At around 5.30 p.m. Mrs Gwen Freeman, Sid's mother, was sitting in the back garden of their bungalow, weaving a tapestry. Sid, meanwhile, was at the front, working diligently to clear a flowerbed of weeds. Suddenly, Gwen noticed the family dog cowering and watched as it ran into the kitchen, its tail tucked between its legs.

Seconds later her attention was caught by what she later described as a strange cloud of light which enveloped her and then, for a split second, actually blinded her. Then, directly in front of her, less than five feet away, a forsythia bush began to shimmer with sparkling lights.

Her attention was caught next by a beam of light which flowed upwards from the bush, travelled between two fir trees and passed over the roof of the garden shed. Gwen followed the beam skywards where it led to a silvery shape, hovering over her house. Stepping to the side she was able to get a better view of the object, realising as she did so that she was confronting a truly awesome phenomenon.* It looked like a some sort of 'spaceship'. Gwen later described it as a large, bulbous-shaped object with a long tail. Beneath the tail section, a light illuminated five V-shaped ports. As she observed this, the front of the 'spaceship' lit up and she noticed that a lip or flange surrounded the circular area. Suddenly the port lights were extinguished and the whole object began to rock from front to back.

* Subsequent events suggest that this encounter had a profound effect on the Freemans. After the incidents described above, Gwen began to exhibit the power to heal by touch, an ability known to have been developed by some individuals following a UFO encounter. Indeed, from Gwen's description of her experience, and such images as the 'burning bush', the evidence for a spiritual dimension to this case is striking.

Gwen then shouted to Sid: 'You'll never guess what I'm looking at! Come quickly before it goes'.

Anxious to find out what had caused so much excitement, Sid hurried to the fence that separated the front and back gardens. Unfortunately, he paused for a split second before following Gwen's finger, pointing skywards. The object was now rapidly diminishing in size and intensity. A bright flash followed, and the UFO was gone.

At this point Gwen's husband, Sid senior, arrived on the scene. He had not witnessed the encounter, as he had been gardening directly in front of the bungalow out of sight of both Gwen and the hovering object. From where he knelt the 'spaceship' was hidden from view by a cluster of trees. Sid, however, was intrigued by the incident and together the family attempted to estimate the size of the object Gwen and her son had seen. They judged it to be around one hundred and fifty feet in length, floating about eighty feet above the ground. They all agreed that in shape it reminded them of a Yale key.

The family decided to call in the local police, and two officers soon arrived. One remarked to his colleague, perhaps not intending Sid to hear, that the 'Yale key' sounded just like an object that had already been reported over Blairgowrie. The officers then moved outside and searched the garden, taking soil samples from the area where Mrs Freeman had been sitting, and collecting leaves from the forsythia bush. After about two hours, the policemen left, telling the family that they would keep them informed of the outcome of the investigation. In fact, from that day to this the Freemans have not heard one more word from the police. Why, it may be asked, the secrecy? Attempts in the early 1990s by UFO investigator Ken Higgins to locate police reports of the incident met with no success. No-one at the police station remembered the incident, and Ken was informed that any documents relating to it would have been transferred and probably destroyed.

But the family's strange encounter was to be only the start of a sequence of unexplained events. One morning Sid and Gwen heard an unusual rumbling above the house. The noise grew louder until it became deafening, and the whole bungalow seemed to vibrate. Looking from the back door, they were shocked to see a large military helicopter hovering some forty feet above the house. Underneath it were slung two box-like devices, one black and the other orange. They were hanging so close to the roof that Gwen could see a small red light on one of the boxes. It seemed that the crew were filming the area around the Freeman home. From the way the helicopter was moving they got the distinct impression that it was also testing the air. In the light of the family's recent encounter, if it was a coincidence, it seemed a remarkable one indeed.

Sid phoned the nearest RAF station, Leuchars, to find out just what was going on. After some initial difficulty, he was informed that the helicopter was simply 'on manoeuvres', and that there was nothing for the family to worry about. Two days later, however, they were startled by the reappearance of the helicopter and were struck by the fact that it repeated the earlier tests. Significantly, the RAF had not chosen Blairgowrie previously to carry out exercises, nor have they found it a suitable spot since.

When Ron Halliday visited Sid in the summer of 1991, shocking new details of the events of 25th April 1984 began to emerge. Some time before midday, Mrs Freeman had called her son to the window, and they both watched in silence as a group of strangely dressed men walked quietly up the deserted street. The sight was remarkable: some twelve men, all dressed in black, wearing hats of the same colour and several with pigtails stretching down their backs.

Sid's curiosity, however, turned to anxiety when the group of strangers walked up the path of a neighbour's house, then disappeared inside without even bothering to ring the doorbell. Gwen was struck by one other odd fact. The twelve had kept moving in single file, a regular space between each one, from the moment they had caught her attention to the time they entered the next-door bungalow.

Gwen and Sid had no wish to be nosey, but as good friends of the woman next door they were concerned for her safety. Just as they had made up their minds to go and investigate, the same twelve came out of the front door, still in single file, and walked back the way they had come. Convinced that something odd had taken place, Sid and Gwen decided to make sure that nothing had happened to their friend.

They rang the doorbell, then waited anxiously. The door was soon opened by their friend, who seeing their worried faces asked what the matter was. Taken aback, Sid explained why he and Gwen had called round, describing the strange figures they had seen on her garden path. It soon became clear that, as far as she was concerned, no-one, and certainly not any mysterious men in black, had entered her house either that or any other day. On hearing this, the Freemans were staggered, embarrassed and worried. Muttering apologies, Sid and Gwen hurried home.

Accounts of mysterious 'men in black', or MIBs as they are known, are by no means uncommon in UFO-related cases. In *Fact or Fantasy*, Hilary Evans discussed several such cases. Typical is one that occurred in September 1976, involving Dr Herbert Hopkins of Maine, USA, who was acting as a consultant in an alleged UFO case. He was telephoned by a man claiming to be a UFO investigator, who shortly afterwards arrived at his door dressed completely in black. The visitor behaved in such a strange way that Hopkins 'was very much shaken' by the incident. The Freeman case has similarities to Dr Hopkins' tale—a UFO event associated with the appearance of odd individuals in black—but it is interesting to note that the Blairgowrie men in black were seen *before* the UFO incident, rather than after it. Whoever they were, and whatever the purpose of their visit, the appearance of MIBs in Blairgowrie on the same day as the UFO encounter is, at the very least, an extraordinary coincidence.

FILE NO: 006
SUBJECT: .... Close Encounters/windowed craft
LOCATION: .... Glasgow/various
DATE: 1976, 1983
CLASSIFICATION: .... CEI
STATUS: .... open

THE FLYING RAILWAY CARRIAGE

Are alien spaceships visiting Glasgow? After his experience, Tom Coventry, for one, is convinced that they are. His close encounter took place on the morning of 15th December 1983.

Tom left for work at about 6.25 a.m., and followed his usual route down Menock Road in the King's Park district. It was a crisp, dry morning, weather which boosted Tom's spirits as he had a bus to wait for at a stop with no shelter in which to escape from any sudden downpour. As he stood there, his attention was caught by a distant object moving in his direction at low altitude. At first Tom thought it was an aircraft moving in a wide arc. Then he noticed spurts of flame issuing from the rear and wondered if it was in some kind of trouble, but as it came nearer, it dawned on him that this was not an aircraft.

All around him things seemed to become strangely quiet. The object that now passed right over his head and hovered not more than twenty feet away was like nothing he had seen before.

'It was coloured grey,' reported Tom, 'shaped like a railway carriage, but with a curved roof'. From it there came crackling and humming sounds—like electricity. Being so close, Tom could easily make out three porthole shaped windows at the front through which he could see an interior swirling with yellow smoke.

Slowly the object moved off towards a nearby railway bridge. There it stopped for a second, then shot skywards vertically before heading across the city. Tom watched it disappear into the distance, and as he did so, the strange silence that had descended around him when he first saw the UFO came to an end.

Equally strange, however, to Tom, was the fact that no-one else seemed to have witnessed the incident even though a bus arrived while the object was still clearly visible. Infuriating, too, was the absence of the milkman who Tom always saw at that time on his rounds, except that morning! It was the one time he failed to turn up.

Tom's encounter was not the first time a 'flying railway carriage' had been reported. As far back as 1916 a Royal Flying Corps pilot flying over southern England, on the lookout for enemy zeppelins, spotted 'a row of what appeared to be lighted windows which looked something like a railway carriage with the window blinds drawn.' This incident occurred over Essex on a dark January night, so the pilot's view of the UFO was by no means as clear as Tom's. Unlike Tom, he was not fascinated by what he saw, but shot at it with his pistol, and the UFO immediately vanished.

Tom Coventry's encounter also echoes, in a number of ways, another incident which occurred in Glasgow. One night in May 1976, Allistair McNeil and two friends were sitting chatting in his flat in Westbourne Gardens, when a movement outside caught his attention. Looking out, he saw what he described as a large, silvery, disc-shaped object, which was hovering about 100 feet above a stretch of grass opposite.

Both he and his friends witnessed this object. It was reported as being around 60 feet in diameter, with round porthole windows on the upper sections, through which light was shining. The object was a silvery colour, and emitted a buzzing and humming noise—sounds very similar to those reported eight years later by Tom Coventry. After a moment, the object seemed to move swiftly towards them, before climbing rapidly out of sight.

FILE NO: 007
SUBJECT: .... alien landing/hostile activity
LOCATION: .... nr. Dunblane
DATE: .... 1992 onwards
CLASSIFICATION: .... CEII, FB5
STATUS: .... open

ALIEN INTRUDERS

Is it possible that UFOs regularly use an area of Scotland as a landing ground?

One man is convinced, through his own observations, that this is exactly what they do. He is David Evans, an active 70-year-old living near Dunblane, a few miles north of Stirling. From a hill directly behind his home, Mr Evans has witnessed the movements of dozens of 'flying saucers', as he unashamedly labels them.

Mr Evans's story is an extraordinary one, even in the annals of ufology, which is itself a history of the bizarre. Knowing that there are many who are only too willing to ridicule his claims, he has sought to obtain evidence to back up what he has seen in the surrounding hills. He has taken dozens of photographs of the alleged landing site, several of which, he claims, show UFOs and the methods used by the 'saucers' to defend themselves.

David's experiences started during 1992, when he was involved in a close encounter with a 'spaceship'. What he describes as an 'alien craft' travelled from the hill overlooking his garden, and continued towards the village, before disappearing from view behind the high ground beyond. Because it passed so close, he had a good view of the object. He was struck by the grid-like 'mesh' that seemed to form a protective skin enveloping the vessel. It was metallic, or appeared so, glistening in the sun as it passed over his head.

David Evans, being the character he is, did not let the matter rest there, nor did he run to the press with a sensational story. Instead, he decided to carry out his own investigation to see if he could find out where this UFO had come from. He was to be staggered by the facts that emerged.

Perched on the summit of the hill overlooking his home, David kept a watch on the mountains which surround the village where he lives. He watched and waited, certain that, sooner rather than later, an object would reveal itself and confirm what his instincts told him.

It was, however, an incident much closer to home that convinced him that he was on to something extraordinary. One night in his sitting room he became aware of a strange glowing light. It seemed to be penetrating far into the kitchen from the paved back-yard.

Carefully, he made his way into the kitchen and, standing well back, looked through the double-glazed door into the yard. Unfortunately, he could not make out clearly the source of the mysterious light.

Cautious enough not to open the door for a closer look, David crept into the bathroom from which a window overlooked the spot where the light was coming from. He turned on the bathroom light then headed back to the kitchen, hoping that he might now get a clearer view of whatever was outside. In that short space of time, however, the light outside had disappeared. This unexpected visitation convinced David that in his surveillance activities he was on the right track. The watchers knew they were being watched.

Even when an alien presence apparently entered his house David was not put off his pursuit. Although he didn't see the object on this occasion—'they were too smart for me this time', was his verdict—the intruder left tell-tale signs which David was quick to latch on to.

While he was in the garden, he heard a strange humming sound coming from inside the bungalow. When he looked inside, he discovered a round depression formed in the carpet with the pile distinctly pressed down. It seemed as if a small yet heavy object had recently rested there.

Perhaps, he reasoned, the object had not actually made contact with the carpet, but moved on a cushion of pressurised air. The force might be strong enough to make a permanent impression on a soft covering. Whatever the explanation, there was no doubt in his mind that the mark had been produced in some inexplicable way. David knew that he had not been responsible for it.

From then on, David made frequent and increasingly determined efforts to photograph the 'flying saucers'. He succeeded, he believed, on a number of occasions. But these photographs, rather than providing a solution, simply added to the mystery. According to David, the UFOs deliberately 'spiked' his photographs, so that the pictures of the mysterious objects he had caught on film were blotted out by a peculiarly shaped, multi-coloured form—as if some strange object had rushed by just as David's finger pressed the shutter.

To David, the fact that his pictures were deliberately obscured was further proof that he was dealing with an intelligence of some kind. The objects, he argued, had been sent by a controlling 'mother' ship. As in the Bob Taylor case [*see File No. 001*], they could well have been remote-controlled devices, sent out to protect the UFO from prying eyes.

Whilst no-one can doubt David's sincerity on the matter, it has to be said that others have offered straightforward explanations to account for the photos David has taken. To at least one professional photographer, the prints show only a reflection caught by the lens. David vehemently dismisses such a mundane solution and points out that the strange mark appears on the negatives neither before nor after the ones on which it is seen.

David also argues that the UFOs have the ability to merge into the background, and can adapt their form to that of the surrounding area. That explains why it is difficult to spot a

UFO which has, for example, landed on a hillside—because it can camouflage itself to an extraordinary degree. A report of a UFO incident which occurred in July 1975 near Machynlleth, Powys, suggests that Mr Evans' explanation for a UFO's invisibility may not be so far-fetched. According to the witness to the 1975 sighting 'the light on top of the object and inside the base began to glow and pulsate in a strange mixture of colours that exactly matched the scenery . . . it simply went into the background like a chameleon camouflaging itself . . . after a few moments it was not there any more!'

If there truly are alien craft using this remote Scottish glen as a base, is it possible they could be aggressive and even be prepared to destroy one of our terrestrial aircraft? David Evans has no doubt about this—indeed, he is sure it has already happened.

One May morning in 1993 *The Scotsman* newspaper reported: 'The crash of an RAF Hercules near Blair Atholl, in which all nine on board were killed, was caused by a low altitude stall, an accident report said last night'. But Mr Evans had a completely different view of the matter.

On the afternoon of the disaster he had been out walking in the hills near the town of Comrie. An ex-army man, he is familiar with aircraft sounds.

'A big one went over', he later told Ron Halliday, 'I could tell by the noise it was making. I knew it wasn't a jet'.

As the sound of the engines receded, David watched as one of the disc-shaped UFOs, by now well known to him, passed above the hilltops. Later that evening David learned of the Hercules crash and guessed its cause. The UFO, suspecting that the Hercules had been sent to monitor its activities, had destroyed it to warn off further interference.

That night, David rang Ron Halliday and informed him of his theory. Initially, Ron was sceptical. It seemed too incredible a story to be true, like something out of a 1950s science-fiction comic. However, given such a mind-bending story, it was necessary to do it justice and, consequently, Ron did enquire at Glasgow Airport, who referred him to Prestwick, about aircraft movements in the area. He was told that there were none that could not be properly accounted for. Whatever David had seen, it could not have been another aircraft.

After further investigation, it emerged that there had been three Hercules aircraft travelling in the same direction, but each following a separate route. One of the routes did seem near enough to Comrie for David to have heard the noise of its engines. It seemed that here was independent confirmation that David could possibly have heard the Hercules passing at the location and at the time he claims.

A hillwalker also witnessed the aircraft's presence, although, at the time, David did not think of taking the man's name. If he were to come forward now, it would provide vital additional evidence in support of David's strange observation. Until that time, and in the absence of further information from the MoD, the precise details of the incident are likely to remain shrouded in mystery.

FILE NO: 008
SUBJECT: .... First Close Encounter
LOCATION: .... nr. Edinburgh
DATE: 1947–present
CLASSIFICATION: .... CEI, CEIII
STATUS: .... open

THE DAY IT ALL BEGAN . . .

Scotland's earliest reported UFO sighting took place in July 1947. Andrew Cherry was a 22-year-old factory worker, employed by Woods Bottle Works in the Portobello district of Edinburgh. His encounter began at 5.30 a.m. on a beautiful summer's morning, as he waited at his usual bus stop, close to St John's School in Baileyfield Road.

Glancing skywards, he caught sight of a strange object, disc-shaped with what looked like a large, glass dome in the style of an observation window. The UFO was hovering about 300 feet above the ground, close enough for Mr Cherry to get a clear view of its humanoid occupant. The 'alien' was wearing dark clothes and was sitting or standing beside a control panel of some kind. He also noted the marked metal texture of the spacecraft—'like rough diamonds'—and the 'orange-yellow colour', which he thinks may have been simply a reflection of the sun's rays.

The area around the object looked hazy, possibly owing to the object's energy source. Mr Cherry could hear a low, smooth hum, which he associated with the flames he could see escaping from the disc. He reckoned it to be 12 to 15 feet in length, but showing tremendous power as it tilted, spun away and disappeared over the Fife coast in a matter of seconds. Mr Cherry describes his experience as 'ghostly, eerie and awesome'.

This extraordinary event made such a profound impression on Mr Cherry that he has never forgetten what he saw. As he said in 1994, 'after all this time I still have chills run through my body'.

Almost half a century later, Portobello was to witness another extraordinary UFO encounter. One morning in October 1992, Pat Macleod was driving along Duddingston Park on her way to the local health centre to keep an appointment. The time was 9.50 a.m. As she drove, Pat became aware of an extremely bright flashing light in the sky. Half a mile further on, keeping the light in view, she realised that it was getting bigger and the brightness intensifying. In fact it seemed to be drawing much closer to her and as it approached she noted that the central sphere of light had a ring or flange round it. This reminded her of pictures she had seen of the planet Saturn.

At about twenty to thirty feet from the ground, the object slowed down and appeared to hover. It was large. Very large.

The length of an aircraft wingspan, according to Pat. Around the circumference, at regular intervals, were squares of light, like glowing windows.

Pat estimates it was now around ten o'clock. She was due at the health centre at that time, and she arrived not too long after. As she turned off the main road, the object veered east in the opposite direction and slowly descended, seeming to land in an area of open ground called Niddrie Burn: a valley-shaped expanse of grass with a stream running through it. This area is surrounded by houses and multi-storey flats which have a clear view of the place where the UFO apparently came down. Incredibly, in spite of considerable publicity over the incident, not a single person came forward to testify to having seen the object at the time of Pat's sighting. Pat confirmed that there were cars on the road at this time, though they were heading away from the descending UFO.

How is it possible that something so large and bizarre, so utterly distinctive, could be seen by Pat, but pass unnoticed by others? Did Pat misidentify another natural object? Investigation into the possibility that this might be a helicopter initially proved inconclusive. Although evidence indicated that there had not been any helicopter movement in that area at the time, it is impossible to be certain. But Pat obviously knows a helicopter when she sees one and is adamant that, whatever she saw, it was not a helicopter. She was able to confirm that the object she saw moved silently, which casts further doubt on the helicopter theory. Furthermore, such a machine landing near Niddrie Burn in broad daylight would surely have been spotted and reported. A helicopter as the basis of this incident must therefore be ruled out, particularly if we accept that the object passed within a hundred feet of her car and Pat had every opportunity to make a positive identification. She was so convinced something weird had happened that she called the police to enquire whether any other witness had rung in to report the event. Then, as now, Pat was determined to prove the reality of what she saw. A number of people later came into the shop she owned and confirmed that they too had witnessed strange incidents at the time of her encounter. Not being an experienced investigator of UFO phenomena, Pat did not bother to take their names, an omission she later regretted.

UFO sceptic Steuart Campbell has a completely different explanation for Pat's encounter. He believes that she saw a double-merged mirage of Mercury, enlarged via a temperature inversion.* Mr Campbell points out that Mercury would have been in Pat's line of sight as she drove down Duddingston Park South. He suggests that Pat's description of the object as 'resembling Saturn' is 'a good description of a double-merged mirage of a planet'. Pat's movement in the car may then have created the impression that the object was growing in size and 'landing'. Although this explanation cannot be dismissed, the intense nature of the experience coupled with Pat's detailed observation of the object at close quarters would seem to rule out this scientific explanation.

* See *The UFO Mystery Solved*, by Steuart Campbell, 1994.

Interestingly, however, though no other witnesses directly confirmed Pat's sighting, evidence did emerge of curious events that day which back up Pat's account. Jon Jeromsom, who ran a plumbing business in Duddingston Park, was looking out of his showroom window when he saw a bright object descend to about 50 feet. It hovered for several seconds, then vanished. This happened at 10 a.m.—exactly the same time as the object Pat had encountered disappeared from her view. Later that day Mr Jeromsom believes he observed the same light again, hovering over a building directly opposite his business at around 4.45 p.m.

Portobello did not have to wait another fifty years before the next UFO was reported. On Christmas Day 1992 Mrs Ann McGuire of Portobello High Street looked out of her bedroom window at 10 p.m., and became aware of a black oval-shaped UFO in the night sky. She had a good view of the mysterious object as it stood clear of clouds and was sharply defined. She watched it for three minutes, during which time it remained stationary. It made no noise and she was not aware of the object moving away. Later that week when she saw a drawing of Pat's UFO in the *Edinburgh Evening News* she instantly recognised it as the one she had seen. If Mrs McGuire's identification was correct, then we are left with an intriguing, and so far unanswered, question: why had the same UFO returned to Portobello twice in the space of three months?

FILE NO: 009
SUBJECT: ....fireball encounters
LOCATION: ....Shetland/Cumbernauld
DATE: 1992/1996
CLASSIFICATION: ....CEI, CEII, MA1
STATUS: .... open

FIRE IN THE SKY

On 6th January 1992, Arthur Moar, a retired farmer from the Shetland town of Sandwick, 15 miles south of Lerwick, rose early as usual. It was still pitch dark when he became aware of a bright flashing light outside. Rushing to the window to see what it was, he saw an object on the ground some 40 yards from the house. He could hardly believe his eyes—the object emitting this strange pulsing light was unlike anything he had ever seen before. Grey and red in colour, it was around six feet high and surrounded with flame. In the centre was a glowing globe, which appeared to be made of a suede-like material, and on which he could clearly make out the outlines of the countries of the world. The bright flashing light seemed to be coming from a tube at the back of the object.

Almost immediately, the mysterious object rose and disappeared, leaving the solid light tube behind on the ground, but this soon dematerialised leaving no trace of its presence.

At first sight this appears to be a startling account of a close encounter with a UFO. Yet without other witnesses or photographic evidence it is hard to be sure what took place that morning. Mr Moar's seemingly bizarre experience, however, is by no means unique—a series of unexplained events that began in Cumbernauld four years later bears a striking resemblance to his encounter.

The experiences of Paul, a public sector worker, began one October morning in 1996. He had set off to work as he did each day, driving to the outskirts of Cumbernauld. As he turned left from a junction on to the main Glasgow road he caught sight of a strange object hovering low down over a clump of trees. It was just before 6 a.m., and Paul parked the car at the side of the road to watch the UFO. He described the object as shaped like a ship's keel, although a drawing he made of the incident shows an object that might have been a disc shape viewed from an off-axis angle. At each side of the UFO there was a dull, red, glowing light. He found it difficult to estimate its size.

This sighting had a profound effect on Paul. He was convinced that if he had managed to catch a glimpse of one UFO, there must be others moving around the area, and he was determined to photograph one of them. Although almost every witness to a UFO incident is amazed by what they have seen, it is extremely rare for one person to experience such encounters time and time again. Individuals who fall into this group are labelled 'repeaters' and there are very few to be found in Scotland. Paul is one of them.

From the balcony of his house, which commands a good view of the valley below and tree-lined hill beyond, Paul began to notice strange balls of light, not only around the sky, but also over the houses and factories within a mile or two of his own home. Paul emphasises that these UFOs are 'not big ones, but small, silver-coloured ones, undetectable unless you are looking for them'. Some of these objects will actually sit on top of buildings, and according to Paul, who has followed them through his binoculars, chase after cars and planes. He has seen them landing in fields and shooting upwards into the sky.

In January 1997 events took a new twist when one of the objects, which had been perched on a factory less than a mile away, flew up to the window of his home. Although the object was small, about two feet across according to Paul, it was a spectacular sight. He had no feeling that this was intended as something specifically for him, nor was he convinced that it was aware of his presence. He has no sense of having some special contact with an alien presence, which makes his claimed experiences all the more remarkable.

There is no doubt, however, that Paul has experienced some very close encounters. Whilst some of Paul's alleged UFO sightings may well have a natural explanation, such as distortions produced by binoculars, a number of his encounters fall within the typical parameters of an 'unexplained' incident.

At 2.20 on this January morning, while Paul was lying awake in his bedroom in the early hours, he caught sight of a cone-shaped object moving in the skies above Cumbernauld. He jumped out of bed and rushed downstairs to grab his camera. But when he pressed the shutter release button, the camera appeared to jam. Paul immediately assumed that he had run out of film, but when he looked at the dial he saw that it displayed the number 16, indicating that there were several more frames left. Thinking that the camera batteries might be flat, he swapped them for the ones in the TV remote control. But when he stepped on to the balcony to photograph the UFO the camera still refused to work. (It is worth noting that failure of electrical equipment is commonly reported during UFO encounters.)

A number of shining objects were now visible. One had come right up to the house and was hovering just below the gutter. The other objects were rotating above the fields directly opposite the housing estate. Paul found himself fascinated by the one that seemed to have attached itself to his house. As he later reported: 'I couldn't take my eyes off it'. As he watched, a strange feeling came over him. He felt intense vibrations, but these came from inside his body—as if his internal organs were being stirred up. Paul suddenly became aware of how alone and isolated he was and stepped off the balcony back into his living room, closing the glass sliding door behind him.

Hardly had he sat down to recover when his wife shouted to him from the bedroom: 'Are you still up? It's half past five!'

Paul glanced at his watch. She was right. He hurried upstairs. It was only later that the chilling thought struck him: where had three hours of his life gone? Everything that had happened since 2.20 a.m. could only have taken minutes, at the most possibly half an hour. Yet it was undoubtedly true that a whole three hours had elapsed.

Paul's story, while unusual, does contain elements in common with many UFO encounters—for example, the 'missing time' which he noted on that January morning. But as yet, no explanation has been put forward for this extraordinary sequence of events in the skies over Cumbernauld.

McX
010

FILE NO: 010
SUBJECT: .... radar tracking of UFOs
LOCATION: .... Aberdeen/Edinburgh
DATE: 1991/1995
CLASSIFICATION: .... DD, RV
STATUS: .... open

AIRPORT UFOs

One of the most convincing UFO sightings in recent years happened at Aberdeen Airport on the 9th November 1991. At around midday, an air traffic controller, John Holmes, looked out of the window and saw something unusual hovering close to the airfield. He is usually able to identify all sorts of flying objects, viewed from any angle, but this one baffled him. To get a closer look, he reached for his binoculars, but despite getting a much better view, he was still unable to make any sort of positive identification.

Holmes called the main tower and asked them to check it out, but the object was not visible from their position. The tower controller said that he would check the radar and call him back. In the meantime Holmes called his colleagues in the same building, asking them to come and see the mysterious object. Only a few minutes at most had elapsed since he first saw the object, but by the time his colleagues arrived, the UFO had started to move away rapidly. Although they confirmed that they could see something, it was by now too far away to get any clear idea of what it might be. Then the tower controller called back to say that nothing unusual had shown up on the radar—there were the usual aircraft circling the airport, and even one small plane coming in to land at the time of his sighting, but the pilot had reported nothing unusual.

So what could this object have been? John Holmes claimed that the object he had seen was cube-shaped, and although there have been similar shapes of UFO reported before, they are unusual. 'Flying saucers' are typically imagined as disc or oval-shaped, but square-shaped UFOs have been reported. In October 1996, for example, Margaret Dewar of Sauchie near Alloa spotted a strange object that looked like a flying box as she looked out of her sitting room window. The object was moving slowly and making no noise. Checks with Edinburgh Airport confirmed that no aircraft were in the area at the time.

The most obvious explanation for an object which hovered for a while before moving off would either be a helicopter or a hot-air balloon, but there are good reasons why these explanations are unsatisfactory in this case. Firstly, any helicopters in the area would have shown up on radar, and it is extremely unlikely that a helicopter could have penetrated the airport's airspace undetected. Secondly, the balloon theory, although seemingly plausible, has several important flaws. At the time of the sighting there was little wind, and certainly not enough to carry a balloon such a large distance in the short space of time between Holmes's first sighting and the arrival of his colleagues. And although there are many strange-shaped hot-air balloons in existence, John Holmes maintains that there was definitely no basket or similar structure suspended beneath the object he saw.

The following day, Holmes was still mystified by the sighting and decided to follow it up himself. But his enquiries at the major military radar centres yielded no further information—there had been no reports of anything unusual the previous day.

The sighting that day remains a mystery, but there is no doubt in Holmes's mind that he saw something which, despite his expertise in the field, is currently beyond his or anyone else's power to explain.

A similar case occurred at Edinburgh Airport in April 1995. A commercial airline pilot, Iain Ray, brought his cargo into Edinburgh Airport from the East Midlands. It was a regular run and he had landed on time at 1 a.m. It had been a clear night and the flight had been trouble free. As Ray taxied off the runway away from the passenger terminal, he noticed a lot of excitement among the British Airways security staff. He learned that Air Traffic Control radar systems had monitored an unidentified flying object hovering near the airport. There had also been a visual sighting confirming the presence of the UFO. As Air Traffic Control followed the

UFO's movements, a cargo plane from a Newcastle-based company was coming in to land. Edinburgh asked the pilot to take a look at the strange object, but he was unable to confirm the report. On the ground, though, there seem to have been several well-qualified witnesses to the presence of an unidentified flying object.

Or were there? A week later, Iain Ray was back in Edinburgh and asked Air Traffic if they had reached any conclusion about the mysterious visitor. He was met by a wall of silence. The tower denied all knowledge, claiming they didn't know what he was talking about. Mystified, Ray mentioned it to colleagues. And then an even stranger tale emerged. He was told that on the same night RAF Kinloss had scrambled three Tornado aircraft to investigate objects which appeared as bright white lights at an altitude of two to three thousand feet. As the fighters approached, these objects shot straight upwards and disappeared. When Ron Halliday of SEMR attempted to confirm this incident, he met with a firm, but extremely speedy, denial from the Ministry of Defence.

Whether or not these UFOs were visitors from another planet, something strange was seen over Edinburgh that day, and, for some unknown reason, the authorities later felt it necessary to withhold any evidence of such an event ever having taken place.

FILE NO: 011
SUBJECT: .... covert military testing
LOCATION: .... throughout Scotland
DATE: 1990s
CLASSIFICATION: .... DD, FB1, CEI
STATUS: .... classified

BEYOND THE AURORA PROJECT

The covert activities of the Ministry of Defence are often shrouded in mystery. Government spokespersons frequently refuse to confirm military aircraft movements, and routinely deny the existence of highly secret projects, while the Official Secrets Act hampers all attempts at investigation. This obsession with secrecy only adds to the concern felt by those who report strange phenomena to the authorities, and receive in return nothing but vague official statements denying all knowledge of any such events.

Over the years, a number of seemingly diverse cases have come to light, particularly in remote parts of Scotland, which raise the question of possible military involvement in UFO sightings.

Writing in *Phenomenal News* in 1996, John Morrison

described an incident which occurred in the summer of 1993 on the Isle of Lewis. Two police officers were driving along a quiet country road when two bright balls of light flew over them. These lights were apparently silent and were sufficiently unusual to prompt the officers to check with the local airfield. Air Traffic Control reported that they knew of no aircraft in the area at that time. Several days later, however, they reported that there had indeed been an aircraft flying at that time in the vicinity of the policemen's reported sighting. No explanation was given as to why this had not been admitted at the time.

Another report of unexplained bright lights in the sky came from the pilot of a flight from London to Iceland a few months before the sighting by the policemen in Lewis. The flight had begun perfectly normally, but, as they flew over the west coast of Scotland, the pilot noticed that the aircraft was apparently being tracked by two fireballs. The objects stayed with them all the way to Iceland, then, as they approached Reykjavik, the fireballs disappeared towards the horizon.

Also from the Isle of Lewis—this time from Stornoway—comes a third incident involving a fireball in the sky. This time the witness was walking home late one summer evening in 1995 when a 'huge orange oval', which she described as the size of a car, suddenly appeared. She watched, fascinated as it came rapidly towards her and then slowed down and hovered above some houses nearby. It only remained there for a short time, before rising up and disappearing over the horizon at high speed. The story was investigated in detail by the local newspaper, and enquiries to the local Air Traffic Control confirmed that they had no record of any air traffic in the vicinity at that time.

Another report, from Shetland in December 1992, described a bright light in the sky, and was backed up by numerous calls to the police, some describing it as a fireball, others simply as a searingly bright white light, but undoubtedly referring to the same incident. There was even a report of this incident from as far away as Banchory in Aberdeenshire, the caller giving a time which seemed to tie in with Shetland sightings.

At Stenness in Orkney, near the standing stones of Brodgar, Stephen Leech and Paul Anderson reported seeing a light in the sky travelling so fast that in their opinion it could not possibly have been a plane. This sighting was in January 1994 at around half past eight in the morning, and is typical in that it was over very quickly and, although seen by both Stephen and Paul, no other witnesses have come forward to corroborate their story.

These cases, all involving fireballs, have not yet been satisfactorily explained. It has, however, been suggested that these strange events are connected with secret military operations—remote Scottish islands have been a favourite proving ground for the military for many years, and exercises regularly take place there.

A spate of UFO sightings further south, off the west coast of Argyll, may provide more substantial evidence for a link between unidentified aerial phenomena and covert military operations.

In 1993, eerie noises accompanied strange objects as they sped across the sky over Argyll. These sightings were reported to the police and to the local RAF base at Macrihanish.

No explanation was forthcoming, but it is interesting to note that the sightings coincided with a visit by a group of Norwegian reporters, who arrived in Scotland seeking information relating to recent avalanches along the coast of Norway. They were following up claims by the Norwegian authorities that these avalanches had been caused by the sonic boom of a US spy plane operating out of the airfield at Macrihanish. There had also been numerous reports, from isolated fishing villages and farmsteads between Trondheim and Narvik, of sonic booms followed by sudden avalanches.

The media interest in these events alerted aircraft enthusiasts and specialists to the possibility that the air base at Macrihanish was being used as a test site for a new aircraft. The MoD admitted that a sonic boom might cause landslides and avalanches, but they refused to comment further on any possible source of such a noise.

Macrihanish is an isolated place a few miles west of Campbeltown in Argyll. The airfield has a runway which is reputed to be approaching two miles in length—an aspect which, along with its location, makes it an ideal testing ground for the US and its NATO allies. Aircraft operating from the base can be monitored by RAF stations at Benbecula and Fylingdales. There is no doubt, then, that it would be high on the list of possible airfields suitable for testing aircraft technology which the government wanted to keep secret.

For many years, UFO investigators in the USA have monitored unexplained events around Groom Lake, part of the Nellis air base and nuclear testing site in the heart of the Nevada desert. Known as 'Area 51', it is a key military location where, it is claimed, top secret 'Black Project' aircraft—including alien spacecraft—are tested.

Could Macrihanish be Scotland's Area 51? The Scottish base is believed to be the home of the mysterious 'Aurora Project'—a secret military operation to test the capabilities of a new type of 'Black Project' aircraft which can fly at three times the speed of sound. This aircraft has never been photographed, and the US Defense Department denies its existence. However, it is worth remembering that the US Air Force made similar denials regarding the now well-known 'Stealth' aircraft—the F117A fighter and the B2 bomber. It is more than likely that the unique radar-defying shape of these aircraft will have given rise to numerous reports of UFOs, as their contours are not like those of other known aircraft.

One particular event which occurred in October 1996 remains unexplained, but may well be linked to military operations. On Saturday 26th October at 4.10 p.m. a huge explosion was reported off the northern tip of the island of Lewis, an area known as the Butt of Lewis. Few people live in this wild and remote spot some twenty miles north of Stornoway, but there were several witnesses to this incident.

They described a huge flash of light in the sky and a loud bang, followed by a trail of smoke leading into the sea. One witness also claimed to have seen an object flying high in the sky just before the explosion occurred. There were, however, no reports of any civilian aircraft in trouble in the area, so could this have been an incident involving an experimental military aircraft?

Also currently unexplained is an event which seems to have occurred all over Scotland on the morning of the 23rd September 1997. Reports of a loud explosion and orange, red and white lights flashing across the sky were received by the police, the coastguard and the RAF. At first, the most likely explanation seemed to be many people witnessing an aircraft in trouble. But it soon became clear that with similar reports being received from areas as diverse as the Outer Hebrides, the east coast of Scotland, the Moray Firth and the Borders that this could hardly be sufficient explanation.

Rescue teams were scrambled to search the areas where incidents had been reported, but they found nothing unusual. Further checks revealed that no aircraft, either military or civilian, had been reported missing over UK airspace at that time. So what was this strange 'sonic event' that had caused so many people to reach for the phone in panic?

Scientists at the Geological Survey in Edinburgh reported that some kind of sonic event, centred in the north-east of Scotland around the Moray Firth, had registered on their instruments. Six of the their seismometers had recorded the activity. But if this was not an aircraft, could it have been a meteorite, or even a satellite burning up on re-entry into the Earth's atmosphere?

This seems the most plausible explanation, except that neither the Royal Astronomical Society nor NASA provided any information to back it up. There were, however, reports that a Russian satellite had broken up as it re-entered the atmosphere at this time. If this were the case, it seems highly unusual that no official confirmation was forthcoming. Whether or not secret military aircraft or UFOs are responsible for these unexplained incidents, they will undoubtedly remain a mystery while the current climate of official secrecy prevails.

```
FILE NO: ................................ 012
SUBJECT: ............... triangular UFOs/cover-up
LOCATION: ............................ Ayr/Dundee
DATE: ................................ 1993/1996
CLASSIFICATION: ........................ NL, DD
STATUS: ................................. open
```

COVER-UP OR CONSPIRACY?

In recent years triangular-shaped UFOs have been seen over various parts of Scotland. One such sighting was reported by Margaret Barrie of Ayr, on Scotland's west coast.

A former executive secretary, Mrs Barrie considers herself an unlikely UFO witness. She was no skywatcher before her encounter, but afterwards she wrote that the incident had turned her into 'an almost compulsive sky-gazer'. Like so many witnesses, Mrs Barrie felt 'privileged to have seen such a strange sight'.

On the morning of Friday 6th September 1996 Mrs Barrie stepped into her garden to hang out her washing. It was a good day for drying clothes, with the sun shining and a strong breeze, and only a small scattering of clouds.

Not far from Ayr lies Prestwick Transatlantic Airport.

Several flight paths cross the town of Ayr, and large passenger planes and military aircraft are frequently seen in the skies overhead. Mrs Barrie watched one travel from the airport in a south-westerly direction until it became a barely visible speck on the distant horizon.

Still at the washing line, her eyes were drawn skywards again and she was astounded by what she saw—a large, dark object, 'a bit like a delta-wing type plane, but at the same time not at all like a plane, as the wings were slowly opening and closing'. She was certain that only moments earlier the sky had been empty.

The UFO, which appeared to be descending, gradually stopped at around 300 to 400 feet from the ground. It seemed to hover. 'There was no sound whatsoever,' Mrs Barrie wrote in her report. 'The object was silent. It was "soft" black in colour and, strangely, there was no glint from it, as when sunlight reflects off metal. There was no glass, no obvious contours.'

She watched the UFO for around ten minutes, fascinated by its strange shape and the mysterious manner of its appearance. Then, hoping to get a better view, Mrs Barrie ran indoors to fetch a pair of binoculars from the upstairs bedroom. At the same time, she called to a workman, who was helping to install a new bathroom suite. Unfortunately, by the time she returned to the garden the UFO had moved from its last position. It was now much higher in the sky, and was travelling almost directly upwards. Mrs Barrie continued to observe it as it travelled through a patch of blue between some clouds, until it finally disappeared from view. The time was now exactly 11.45 a.m.

There may, of course, have been other witnesses to Mrs Barrie's remarkable sighting, but none have so far come forward. Ron Halliday initially thought it likely that some form of experimental aircraft was involved—this has often been put forward as a possible explanation of UFOs with a triangular or near triangular configuration. However, his inquiries with Prestwick Airport (sited close to Ayr and housing Scotland's main Air Traffic Control Centre) brought a negative response. It seems, then, that it was not a new type of aircraft that Mrs Barrie saw that day.

Or at least not one that the powers-that-be are ready to admit to. It is interesting to note that, in the publicity following the Gulf War, accounts emerged from the United States of a curious type of target practice undertaken during testing of Stealth aircraft. In order to simulate precision bombing runs over built-up areas, specific targets, such as individual civilian houses, were chosen—though the occupants of these houses were never informed. One such simulated bombing mission was successfully carried out over Las Vegas, paving the way for the devastating attacks on key targets in Baghdad during the Gulf War. Is it possible that such tests have also been taking place over British soil? [*Stealth aircraft—see File No. 011.*] Until the details of Stealth training flights emerged recently, who would have believed that individual homes could have been subjected to this sort of 'attack' by secret military aircraft?

Another case which highlights the unwillingness of the authorities to discuss possible military manoeuvres occurred in Dundee on 24th July 1993. David Anthony from Edinburgh was staying with relatives in the Menzieshill housing estate situated in West Dundee. At 10.30 p.m., a time noted from a television programme he was watching, David, sitting in an upstairs bedroom, caught sight of a bright light in the sky.

He thought at first it must be an aircraft heading for the local airport at Dundee, but quickly realised he was watching no ordinary phenomenon. The light he saw glowed with a strange intensity, and appeared to be moving slowly south, away from and not towards Dundee. The spherical ball of light was low down, perhaps as low as 100 feet above the ground, but began to climb after a time.

Mr Anthony could follow the UFO's progress, as from his vantage point he could see a distance of perhaps 20 miles or more. Eventually, after he had watched the object for several minutes, it began to lose its blinding white glow and became hazy. Then, suddenly, the single light split into two, then again into two groups of three or four lights, all blazing white.

When Mr Anthony made some inquiries the following day, he discovered that the airport at Dundee had closed at 8.30 p.m., so he could exclude the possibility of a plane either landing or taking off from there. But what about military aircraft? The Ministry of Defence refused either to confirm or deny the presence of military aircraft in the area, their standard disclaimer stating that the MoD only looks at 'reports of unexplained aerial phenomena in order to establish whether what was seen is of defence significance. . . . In this particular instance we are not aware of any evidence which would indicate that a breach of the UK's air defences has occurred but have noted your report for our records'.

Mr Anthony was not satisfied by their response, which took him no further down the road to solving the mystery of his sighting, and replied to the MoD that he was only trying to find out whether there were any military aircraft actually in the area at the time. The second response he received was more blunt: 'details of flight paths for aircraft operating out of RAF Leuchars in July 1993 are no longer available. I am afraid, therefore, that it is not possible to answer your question'.

McX 013

FILE NO: 013
SUBJECT: .... Close Encounter/alien abduction
LOCATION: .... nr. Kennoway, Fife
DATE: .... September 1996
CLASSIFICATION: .... CEIII/IV
STATUS: .... unexplained

THE FIFE INCIDENT

The remarkable series of events which occurred close to Kennoway near Leven in 1996 did not start in any dramatic way, but developed from a simple car journey undertaken by two friends, Lyn and Jean, accompanied by a ten-year-old child, to a local shop to buy coffee. It was around 7.30 p.m. on 23rd September, and it was a clear and dry night.

The encounter began when Lyn, who was in the front passenger seat, spotted a bright oval-shaped light low down in the sky. She watched for a few seconds, wondering what it could be, then turned away. When she glanced back, the single light had become two circles of light. Lyn was now intrigued, as the object did not appear to be moving and so, she was sure, could not be a plane and seemed too big to be a helicopter.

Lyn drew Jean's attention to the light and both agreed that it was difficult to account for. A UFO, then, although neither described it as such at this point. Jean, who was driving, slowed the car to a walking pace so that they could get a better view. The object was now to their left and seemed to be hovering behind a farmhouse whose silhouette was visible against the gentle glow. Beams of light seemed to be travelling from the sky to the ground. Suddenly, the field below the UFO was lit up like a firework display, the intensity of the light turning night into day all around them.

The explosion of light ended as dramatically as it had begun. The object, which had remained stationary for so long, now started to move and as it did so Jean and Lyn noticed its triangular shape and that it appeared to have a dome on its uppermost section. The UFO then moved away swiftly, rotating slowly to display small red dots of light.

Understandably bemused, Jean and Lyn nevertheless drove on to the local shop. Jean bought the coffee and they set off on the return journey. But on the way back they were again confronted by the strange object as they passed the site of their original encounter at around 8.20 p.m. They first spotted red lights ahead travelling at great speed, before the object turned and headed directly towards them. A whole battery of lights came on for an instant, and was then extinguished. And then, as suddenly as it had arrived, the UFO disappeared into the night. Lyn noticed that three cars were travelling behind them, although there was no indication that any of their occupants had seen the mysterious object.

Having returned home, the witnesses decided after further discussion to revisit the area of the incident. They were both nervous and intrigued, not to mention anxious to resolve an incident which they could not explain. So, at 9.45 p.m. they drove back, and as they approached the site their attention was caught by a blue glow which was visible just above a wood. A star-shaped object could also be seen pulsating and emitting coloured streaks of light—alternately red, blue and green—in a rapid sequence. Lyn described them as being like torch beams, narrow at the base and widening as they reached upwards. Strange events were taking place, but no-one could have been prepared for what happened next.

Moving among the trees were several small entities, and whatever they were, they were definitely not human. Above them towered a tall individual, its height estimated at around seven feet, who seemed to be in charge of his smaller companions. Understandably frightened, Jean and Lyn turned the car round and drove home.

Although frightened, they were intrigued by what they had seen, and they decided to return and have another look. This time they took a pair of binoculars, lent by Lyn's brother James. As they reached the place where they had last seen the UFO, the blue light was still glowing, but with the binoculars it was now possible to get a much better view. They could see a shimmering ball which appeared to be emitting heat and energy of some kind. It looked amber in colour, with an irregular surface and dark sections. One of these darker sections, situated near the base, seemed to be an opening. The craft did not appear to be resting on the ground, but was hovering or possibly held up by thin supports. It appeared to be rotating and tilting rhythmically.

To the right of the object, but definitely on the ground, lay a circular disc, coloured dark red but possibly reflecting the amber colour of the ball-shaped craft. All around was a hive of activity, as groups of the small creatures transported boxes and tube-shaped objects from the wood towards the craft. Lyn described these beings as having 'very big, dark eyes and with heads too big for their bodies. They didn't appear to have mouths'. The taller 'supervisor' was still visible and the witnesses could make out his brown skin and narrow eyes.

The incident had a terrifying ending, described by Jean: 'Suddenly dozens of bubble-like things came out of the woods and flew across the field towards us. Then they were all around us, about four feet away, motionless. They were all alike. We could see through them and each one had one of these small creatures inside. They had big black eyes and big heads.'

The echoes of this incident have been no less disturbing than the events of that fateful evening. Understandably, all three witnesses have had to live with the fear and confusion brought on by their experiences. Weeks after the incident was over, Lyn began to have dreams about being taken into the craft. Dreams can often surface in the wake of a terrifying ordeal, but, given the content of the dreams in this case, a rather more sinister possibility presented itself: were details of an abduction experience emerging? The witnesses, quite correctly, were wary of undergoing hypnosis. Conscious recall of events is far more reliable as it allows investigators to examine the evidence without the possibility of 'false memory syndrome', which can sometimes occur with hypnotic regression, obscuring the facts of the experience.

The question of what exactly was going on in that Fife wood has to date not been resolved—a classic 'flying saucer' encounter? An attempted abduction? An alien landing? All these are possibilities, but, whatever the true nature of their experiences, the witnesses have been left with indelible memories of an unparallelled sequence of events, the significance of which we can only guess at.

SECTION II

UNEXPLAINED

FILE NO: 014
SUBJECT: ....the Flannan Lighthouse mystery
LOCATION: ....nr. Isle of Lewis
DATE: ....December 1900
CLASSIFICATION: .... n/a
STATUS: .... open

'GOD IS OVER ALL . . .'

The Flannan Isles, or Seven Hunters, a group of seven islands and numerous smaller rocks and skerries, lie some twenty miles west of Gallan Head on the Isle of Lewis.

In the 19th century, the increase in fishing vessels and other shipping in the Atlantic west of the Hebrides led to an awareness of the dangers posed by these uninhabited islands in rough weather, at night-time or in fog. Surrounded by cliffs of up to 260 feet, the islands are nevertheless quite small: even the largest, Eilean Mór, has an area of less than 40 acres. To land on them at all is hazardous; in a storm, it is almost impossible. If a ship was wrecked on them, even if the crew managed to make it to shore, there was little shelter, nothing to eat except sea-birds and a few sheep kept there by the people of Uig and Great Bernera, and little chance of being seen and rescued by passing vessels.

In 1895 the Northern Lighthouse Board undertook to build a lighthouse on the largest island, Eilean Mór. This was a perilous task, involving blasting a landing-place and steps up the rock on both the east and west sides of the island. Cranes and derricks had to be installed, and all the materials for the lighthouse hoisted two hundred feet up the cliffs. The light-tower was to be 75 feet high, and in clear weather its 140,000 candlepower lantern would be visible for 24 nautical miles all around (though considerably less in bad conditions). It took four years for the work to be completed, but in December 1899 the lighthouse was ready. It was manned by a team of four men who worked in rotation, three on Eilean Mór and one on leave in Lewis. Every 20 days, depending on conditions, the relief ship *Hesperus* would arrive from Oban, to take off one man and deposit his comrade, along with any supplies required.

For a year this operation went on without incident. Then, on 15th December 1900, ships in the locality noticed that there was no light visible on the Flannans. For some days before that a strong westerly gale had been blowing in, but by the 15th this had dropped to a fresh breeze. Captain Holman of the *S.S. Archer* nevertheless sent a message by morse to the shore-station that, passing on a course which should have made the signal clearly visible, at midnight on the 15th/16th December, he saw no light.

The *Hesperus* was due at the lighthouse on the 21st,

carrying supplies and the relief keeper, Joseph Moore, who had enjoyed a good spell of weather on Lewis in his fortnight ashore. But when the *Hesperus*, having collected Moore, set out a storm blew up almost at once, and for three days the ship rode it out at sea, some distance from the Flannans. When they approached closer, it was evident that the light was out. Another two days passed, in sight of the lighthouse but in a swell that made a landing too dangerous, during which time the blasts of the ship's foghorn got no response at all. Captain James Harvie even had a rocket fired from the ship, but to no avail. Finally, on the 26th, Joseph Moore was landed at the east landing-place. The *Hesperus* then stood offshore because the swell was still considerable.

The men whom Moore expected to find on Eilean Mór were James Ducat, Donald McArthur and Thomas Marshall. Moore made his way up the steps to the lighthouse enclosure. The gate was properly closed. So too were the doors of the outhouses and the keepers' living-quarters at the foot of the tower. Moore entered the kitchen. It was empty, but the table had been set ready for a meal. There was a chair lying on its back, but otherwise no sign of disturbance. The room, however, had clearly been empty for days. The ashes in the fireplace were cold and the clock above it had stopped. The sleeping-quarters were also empty. Moore was very afraid and uncertain. He returned to the landing-place and signalled for help. Two more men were landed. Together, all three searched all the buildings and the entire island. There was no sign of the missing lightkeepers. The east landing-place was where the previous relief had been effected on 5th December: that was in a tidy condition, and showed no sign of storm damage. The west landing-place, however, was a different matter.

Superficially, nothing seemed out of order. The crane, on its concrete platform 80 feet above sea-level, was unharmed, its jib secured and its barrel and hawser protected from the salt-water by a securely fixed tarpaulin. 40 feet *above* the crane, however, was a box, usually lodged in a nook in the cliff, which contained spare ropes and other equipment for the crane. This had clearly been dislodged and some of the contents thrown out. Some of them were still lying at points nearby on the rocks. Furthermore a large boulder weighing at least a ton appeared to have moved, and the iron railings at the foot of the stone steps had suffered some twisting and breaking.

This still did not explain what had happened to the men. A further investigation of the lighthouse was carried out. It was discovered that Ducat and Marshall's oilskins and boots were missing. These items would normally have been worn when out on the rock in wet weather. McArthur's gear was still in place. The logical explanation seemed to be something like this: during the fierce storms of the days preceding the 15th, Ducat and Marshall had gone out to the west landing-place to check that everything was secure. They had been swept away, perhaps, by a huge wave which had struck the island at a height of some 120 feet. Then McArthur, aware that something had happened, or going in search of his colleagues, had hurried out without his protective clothing and had also been swept or blown into the sea.

Certainly that was Captain Harvie's belief. Having left Moore and two seamen to get the light working again and, if possible, to find some trace of the missing men, the *Hesperus* sailed for Lewis, where Harvie sent a wire to the Secretary of the Northern Lighthouse Board in Edinburgh. 'Poor fellows,' he said in his message, 'they must have been blown over the cliffs or drowned trying to secure a crane or something like that.'

But there were problems with this. One freak wave might be a possibility, but two coming so close together—was that likely? The men were experienced lighthousemen: Ducat had 22 years' experience, Marshall had 5, and though McArthur's age and experience are not recorded he was a Lewisman and therefore well acquainted with the treacherous ocean. Would they have ventured into such a dangerous location as the west landing-place in extreme weather? What could they have done in any case that they had not already done to safeguard the equipment? The state of the lighthouse showed that they had been punctilious in carrying out their duties in every other detail. The lamps in the tower were trimmed and ready for lighting; the oil fountains were full and primed; the lens and other parts were all cleaned and polished. The beds were made; breakfast dishes and utensils had been washed and put away in the kitchen. Everything was immaculately, disturbingly in order.

There was only one peculiar thing: on the steps of the

tower, and in the small office where the log was kept, were traces of an unusual kind of seaweed. What it was doing there could only be guessed at. And then the investigators read the log.

It appeared to have been kept by Thomas Marshall. These were the entries for the days leading up to the 15th, when the *Archer* had reported the absence of a light.

December 12:
Gale N. by NW. Sea lashed to fury. Never seen such a storm. Waves very high. Tearing at Lighthouse. Everything ship-shape. James Ducat irritable.
Storm still raging, wind steady. Stormbound. Cannot go out. Ship passing and sounding foghorn. Could see cabin lights. Ducat quiet. Donald McArthur crying.

December 13:
Storm continued through night. Wind shifted W. by N. Ducat quiet. McArthur praying.

There was no log entry for the 14th. The entries for the 15th read as follows:

Noon. Grey daylight. Me, Ducat and McArthur praying.
1 p.m. Storm ended, sea calm. God is over all.

From the log, then, it seemed that the keepers had all been alive in the afternoon of the 15th. By that stage, by their own account and those of ships and people on Lewis 20 miles to the east, the worst of the storm was over. There might still have been huge waves coming in from the west, but was it feasible that all three men, either together or at different times, had been carried off from the west-landing when they would have been well aware of the dangers of being there? They might, of course, have ventured out after the storm, to check on their equipment, and they might have been caught off guard. But the storm must have been of an intense ferocity judging by the men's behaviour as recorded in the log. Did they regain their spirits by making 'everything shipshape' again and then, in a bitter twist of fate, set out from their shelter to be killed by a freak wave? Or, as some have wondered, did one of the men go insane, kill the others and then himself? No hammers, knives or axes were missing or out of place from the lighthouse, but in such a scenario a man might use a rock, or simply push his comrades to their deaths, then jump himself. Nobody now will ever know, and it remains an uncanny and tragic mystery. The incident caused much public debate, and was commemorated in a poem by William Gibson (1878-1962) which was for years a standard recitation piece in many schools, with its final lines from the point of view of the men who landed and found no sign of their comrades:

> We seemed to stand for an endless while,
> Though still no word was said,
> Three men alive on Flannan Isle
> Who thought on three men dead.

In Hebridean folklore the Flannans had long been held in great respect. Seamen from Lewis would on no account stay overnight on the islands if it could be avoided. A spirit was supposed to haunt the ruined 6th-century chapel of St Flannan on Eilean Mór. Superstitious islanders were not beyond thinking that sea-monsters had been responsible for the men's disappearance; or that huge sea-birds had plucked them from the island and carried them off to sea.

There is one weird footnote. On the night of 15th December, a small boat called the *Fair Wind* was also in the vicinity of the Flannans. Two sailors on board suddenly observed a strange-looking longboat, carrying a number of men, cutting across their path in the direction of the Flannans. They hailed the boat but got no reply. The men in the boat seemed strangely pale, eerily so. The sailors could see their movements as they pulled at the oars of the longboat. What was this mysterious vessel? A boatful of ghosts, as some have speculated? Whatever, the coincidence of the sighting with the day that three men disappeared from the Flannan Isles lighthouse is striking.

FILE NO: 015
SUBJECT: .... haunting of Mary King's Close
LOCATION: .... Edinburgh
DATE: .... 1600s to present
CLASSIFICATION: AN3
STATUS: .... open

'YOU WILL HAVE MORE COMPANY THAN YOURSELVES'

In 1685 George Sinclair, Professor of Moral Philosophy at Glasgow University, published his treatise on witchcraft, spirits and other strange occurrences, titled *Satan's Invisible World Discovered*. It contained numerous examples of supernatural or paranormal happenings from all over Scotland, England and further afield, and was a bestseller in its day. It was reprinted often throughout the 18th century, though more and more as an antiquarian curiosity than because people believed all that was written in it. But there was one story which has reverberated down the centuries right to the present day, concerning a street in the town of Edinburgh, which is still said to be haunted.

Mary King's Close is a very steep, narrow close running

from the High Street down to what used to be the Nor' Loch, but is now Princes Street Gardens. Built in the early 17th century, it still survives although it has long since been built over. Named, probably, after the daughter of a proprietor, Alexander King, it became notorious as a place infested by the plague of 1645, the last great outbreak in Edinburgh, which wiped out thousands of citizens. The Close was in fact sealed off in this year, and food and water passed in from outside to those unfortunates, whether infected or not, who were thus condemned to live on there. It never shook off the ill repute of that time, and was largely abandoned by the end of the century. In the 1750s the City Chambers were constructed above it, and the last inhabitants moved out. But their houses remain more or less intact 250 years later. The exodus was hastened because the Close was also believed to be haunted. In modern times, its unwholesome reputation led to renewed public interest, and by arrangement with the City Council parties could be given guided tours, gaining entry from a door leading down steps from the Chambers, and arriving in due course at the bottom end, which is blocked up, above Cockburn Street. More recently still the commercial possibilities of the Close have been exploited in the form of visits jointly organised by the Council and a local tour company.

In George Sinclair's book, the following case of haunting is recorded:

Around the year 1680, a lawyer, Thomas Coltheart by name, took a house in Mary King's Close and moved in with his family. One Saturday an inhabitant of the Close, seeing Coltheart's maid taking some light furniture into the house, warned her that if she intended living there, 'I assure you, you will have more company than yourselves.' The maid took fright, and informed her mistress that she would not stay there, because it was haunted by a spirit or ghost.

The mistress informed her husband, asking him to reconsider the let, but Coltheart calmed her and said that he had no intention of changing his mind. Indeed, he insisted that they stay in the house that same night, which they did.

The next day, after attending church in the morning, Coltheart felt unwell, and in the afternoon took a nap. His wife sat reading the Bible, having sent the maid out to church (she never came back). Mrs Coltheart glanced up at one point, and saw, by a 'little Chamber Door just over against her', 'the head and face of an old man gray headed with a gray Beard, looking straight upon her' from a cupboard door above the fire. She fainted, and did not come round till she heard the noise of her neighbours opening their doors after church. She roused her husband and told him what she had seen, but he dismissed it as 'some fancy or delusion of her Senses'.

After his wife had gone to bed, Coltheart sat up alone by the fire. He too saw the same old man's head in the same place. He woke his wife, who fell into a passion, and then together they prayed for God's protection. After an hour 'they clearly perceived a young child, with a coat upon it, hanging near to the old man's head.' Terrified, the Colthearts lit more candles and tried to wake their neighbours, but got no answer. As they watched and prayed, another apparition manifested itself: 'a naked Arm . . . in the air, from the elbow downward, and the hand stretched out, as when one man is about to salute another.' It approached as if it sought to shake hands with the lawyer, who retreated into bed with his wife, but the arm followed, 'still after a courteous manner, with an offer of acquaintance'. Now drowned in sweat, the Colthearts prayed more fervently, but to no avail, as next appeared a little dog, 'which after a little time looking about, and towards the Bed, and the Naked Arm, composed it self upon a Chair, as it were with its nose in its tail to sleep.' There followed a cat, which seemed to leap from the door of a small adjoining room, where all the apparitions had come from, and started to play in front of them. 'Then was the hall full of small little creatures, dancing prettily, unto which none of them could give a name, as having never in nature seen the like.'

The Colthearts continued on their knees in bed, there being nowhere left on the floor for them to kneel, and prayed yet again. 'In the time of prayer,' says Sinclair, 'their ears were startled with a deep, dreadful, and loud groan, as of a strong man dying, at which all the Apparitions and visions at once vanished . . . and the house was quiet.'

The Colthearts, understandably, refreshed themselves with a drink after this awful experience, and in the morning went about their business, making no secret to anyone of what had happened to them. However, they did wonder, looking back, why they had not simply unbolted the door and fled, rather than lighting the first candle. They concluded that they had been meant to undergo the trial, and this gave Coltheart the courage to stay on in that house, until the day he died, which as it turned out was not too long in the future.

After going to Corstorphine one day, to hear a sermon, Coltheart was taken ill on the way home, trembling and aching in his joints, and with a pain in his head. Meanwhile, in Tranent, seven miles the other side of Edinburgh, one of his clients, being in bed one morning with his wife, saw a cloud-like figure like a man floating in the room, and was so startled that he jumped out of bed and drew his sword. After a while, he, his wife and a nursemaid to their child all saw the cloud take the definite form of a man walking up and down. 'At last this Apparition looked him fully and perfectly in the face, and stood by him with a ghastly and Pale countenance. At which the Gentleman with great courage said to the Spectre, what art thou? Art thou my dear Friend Thomas Coltheart?' The ghost held up its hand three times, waving and shaking it, and then disappeared. It transpired that at almost this exact time Thomas Coltheart died.

How much of this is credible is of course open to question. Certainly none of it is now verifiable. However, many visitors to Mary King's Close in recent years claim to have seen or felt presences of some kind. The most frequently experienced is the ghost of a little girl, believed to have been a plague victim, to whom an unofficial shrine has built up in a room of one of the old houses. Mediums and clairvoyants have been down the Close and confirmed that the place is full of ghosts of various kinds, mostly from the period of the plague. As to the weird procession of apparitions observed by the Colthearts, a possible connection was made in 1995, as reported in the *Evening News* on 24th June of that year. A Glasgow architect called David Roulston spent an entire night alone in the Close in order to raise money for charity. He took a camcorder down with him, and recorded a mysterious image on film during the course of his stay. As Roulston explained, at one point he felt quite cold. It wasn't until he played back the video at home that he saw what looked like a head on a wall. To him it was like the head of a dog, which just turned and disappeared. It might also be the image of a human head. The student who edited the tape, one Richard Adamson, also claimed there were 'a few supernatural gremlins' on it. There were strange sounds that appeared without reason, and he was convinced that, around the time the 'ghost' was shot, the speech and music changed tracks.

It would seem that some of the old inhabitants of Mary King's Close are still around.

FILE NO: 016
SUBJECT: ....unidentified animal encounters
LOCATION: ....area around Falkirk
DATE: 1997
CLASSIFICATION: AN3
STATUS: ....under investigation

THE TRACKS OF THE BEAST

The area around Falkirk and Bonnybridge has for some years been known as a centre for UFO sightings, but another disturbing catalogue of events has also been unfolding within the rugged countryside of this region.

At around midnight on 14th July 1997 a cyclist near Falkirk came upon what he described as a huge black cat crouching beside the road. Scott Sutherland reported that the animal, only yards from him, stared straight at him before jumping over a hedge and vanishing. 'It was long and thin, was about three feet tall and had triangular ears. It definitely wasn't a dog. I'm sure of that,' he told the local newspaper, the *Falkirk Herald*.

Although shaken by the incident, he went back to the scene later that night with a friend. They saw nothing, but heard powerful growling noises, 'like something out of a Tarzan film,' according to Mr Sutherland. The police were called, but were unable to shed light on the mystery.

However, this appears not to be an isolated sighting. Earlier in the year, a mysterious animal was reported near Plean, a few miles north-west of Falkirk. Greame McPhee was driving towards Stirling when he caught sight of an animal in the undergrowth beside the road. 'It was about three feet tall and black—there was no way it was a dog.'

He stopped the car and went for a closer look. From ten yards away he had a good view: 'It stood up right next to me, and it was a puma. It was black and moved very quickly. There was no mistaking it.' The area was searched by police, but no further evidence of the animal was found.

These events are part of a wider trend, with sightings coming from various parts of the country. A number of people, from the Scottish Highlands and Borders to the moors of Cornwall, claim to have had close encounters with strange animals. These are generally described as big cats—panthers or pumas, although both popular opinion and expert testimony have tended to dismiss such claims as over-imaginative.

Until recently, that is. Analysis in 1997 of footprints found in a clay pit to the south of Bodmin Moor in Cornwall revealed that the prints are almost certainly those of a puma. The prints were studied by zoologists at Newquay Zoo, who succeeded in obtaining a near-perfect match between the paw patterns found near the Moor and those of pumas held in captivity.

Even more disturbing is that the 'Beast of Bodmin' is not alone. Alongside the prints of an adult puma were found those of a cub, clearly showing that not only is there a big cat in Cornwall, but that it is breeding.

This comes only two years after experts from the Ministry of Agriculture had rejected reports of big cats being seen in the wild. It was not thought possible that such animals could flourish, and sightings were generally explained away as cases of mistaken identity, the view being that what had been seen were dogs.

The parallel between the Bodmin case and similar recent evidence from the Falkirk area is striking.

On 21st September 1997, Brian Davidson was fishing alone from the bank of Loch Coulter, set in hilly countryside about five miles west of Plean. It was midday, and visibility was good. As he walked along the shore to find a new location, he saw in his path what he took to be a large black bag. Then, suddenly, the 'bag' moved, revealing itself to be 'a heavily-built black cat', which he recognised as a panther, describing it as at least two and a half feet tall. 'It was too big to be a dog and too low to be a calf.' The creature turned to look at him, before padding away up the bank and into the nearby undergrowth.

Shocked but not deterred, he approached the place where the animal had been. There he found paw marks in the mud, which were clearly not those of a dog. Later that day he returned to the scene with two other anglers, who saw for themselves the strange footprints at the water's edge.

They told the *Falkirk Herald* how they had then gone to a neighbouring farm to make enquiries. The farmer's wife had seen nothing, but described how one of their sheep had been killed one evening a few weeks previously. Her husband had gone to bury it the following day. 'Overnight it had been eaten by something, but we've no idea what. All we do know is that what we put in the hole was more of a carcass than a sheep.'

A few days after the incident, the newspaper visited the scene, in order to photograph the strange prints. Not only had the marks been well preserved, but a number of similar, smaller prints were to be seen. Just as in the Bodmin case, it would appear that a mysterious wild creature is not only surviving but raising a family.

The three Scottish incidents detailed above took place within a radius of only ten miles, but if there are panthers in central Scotland, then it seems inevitable that sightings will increase, and will become spread over a wider area. This has been the case in North America, where destruction of their habitat has forced pumas to venture further afield, and closer to populated areas.

However, if the animals seen in Scotland are indeed panthers, there is no real danger to humans—these cats are shy, cautious and generally nocturnal creatures whose principal prey are rodents, sheep and occasionally deer. The very rare attacks on humans—there have been fifty reported cases in North America over the last century, leading to nine fatalities—have been put down mainly to animals suffering from rabies, one symptom of which is heightened aggression. In each of the Scottish incidents, the animals displayed no aggressive behaviour, and experts agree that there is no need for any action to be taken against them.

The identity of the Scottish creatures has not been confirmed, but whatever they are, the question of their origin remains. Have such animals been roaming freely in the wilds of Fife for centuries, or have they been recently introduced—and if so, from where?

```
FILE NO: ................................... 017
SUBJECT: ........ the big grey man of Ben MacDui
LOCATION: ............................Cairngorms
DATE: .......................... 1800s to present
CLASSIFICATION: ............................ AN3
STATUS: ..................................... open
```

THE GREY MAN

Mountains all over the world often have associations with the spiritual, the unexplained or the downright peculiar. Some are reputedly haunted by legendary beasts or apparitions. The yeti or 'abominable snowman' of Tibet, and Bigfoot in northwest America, are the most famous examples. Scotland's second highest mountain, Ben MacDui in the Cairngorms, which peaks at 1309 metres or 4296 feet, is home to one such creature: the Big Grey Man, or in Gaelic, Am Fear Liath Mór.

Over the years there have been many reports of uncanny and disturbing experiences by mountaineers and walkers on the mountain. These seem always to be restricted to Ben MacDui itself, and not to other parts of the Cairngorm massif. Sometimes people have seen an enormous shadowy figure in the snows (most experiences take place in winter); sometimes strange unnerving noises are heard; occasionally sets of inexplicably large prints are found in the snow. More often than not, an overwhelming feeling of ill-boding grips the unfortunate traveller, compelling them to flee off the hill from an unknown danger. Although it is true that myths are self-perpetuating, feeding themselves on the expectations of those who hear them, in the case of Ben MacDui something more than a myth seems to be at work. The experiences are simply so numerous, so well-documented, and often come from such impeccable sources, that the strangeness of the mountain has to be conceded. What is left is to decide what is the cause of the phenomenon.

Although there are references to the Big Grey Man in Highland legend, these are not frequent and most come only from the 19th century onwards. Indeed, nearly all the documented 'sightings' have occurred in this century. James Hogg, the Ettrick Shepherd, and John Hill Burton, the historian, make brief passing reference to some strange inhabitant of Ben MacDui, and in 1831 Sir Thomas Dick Lauder, in an article in the *Edinburgh New Philosophic Journal,* described witnessing what he believed was an apparition of the so-called Brocken Spectre on the mountain. But the most famous experience occurred in 1891, and was recounted by Professor Norman Collie at the annual general meeting of the Cairngorm Club in Aberdeen, in 1925. Collie was an Aberdeenshire man, who was Professor of Organic Chemistry at the University of London, and a hugely experienced mountaineer who had climbed in the Himalayas, the Alps and the Rockies in his time. But the most terrifying experience of his life, he told the Club, had taken place 35 years earlier on Ben MacDui.

He had reached the summit, which was thick with mist, and was making his descent when he began to hear what he thought were somebody else's crunching footsteps following after him. The steps, however, appeared to be huge strides, three or four times the length of the Professor's own. He stopped to listen, and could hear the noises distinctly. But he could see nothing. 'I was seized with terror and took to my heels, staggering blindly among the boulders for four or five miles nearly down to Rothiemurchus Forest.' Collie concluded that, though he could not understand what he had heard, there was 'something very queer about the top of Ben MacDui' and he would not go back there again by himself.

The story in itself was not remarkable. But Collie's credentials were: a leading scientist, a man of considerable reticence not prone to exaggeration or hysteria, a skilled mountaineer who had spent many lonely hours on many different mountains, had confessed to being overcome with some nameless fear on one of Scotland's biggest hills. Over the next few decades a host of similar stories were told. Individuals such as Peter Densham, who had worked in the Cairngorms during the Second World War and afterwards as a forester, Wendy Wood the Nationalist activist, Dr A. M. Kellas, another Himalayan climber, Alexander Tewnion, the naturalist and photographer, and the blind Dundonian climber Sydney Scroggie, all reported varying kinds of experiences. Most involved hearing footsteps close behind their own; the possibility of these being merely echoes is usually discounted because of their irregularity. Sometimes a strange voice has been heard. And on occasion a huge shadowy figure has loomed through the mist or snow, only to vanish, leaving no trace of its passage.

The most frequently given explanation is that people are seeing a form of the Brocken Spectre, that weird natural effect which *Chambers English Dictionary* describes as 'the shadow of an observer, enlarged and often surrounded by coloured lights, thrown on to a bank of cloud—a phenomenon sometimes encountered on mountain-tops.' But this does not account for the accompanying, or quite separate, footstep noises. Nor does it explain why Ben MacDui, of all Scotland's hundreds of high mountains, is where this so often occurs. There have, of course, been strange and related experiences on other peaks, from the Cuillins in Skye to the hills of Torridon in the north-west. But Ben MacDui's record exceeds all the others by far. Also, when the sounds of steps are dismissed as echoes or the noise of other walkers and climbers, it must be remembered that most of the experiences occurred in the earlier decades of this century, when there were very few people on the hills at all, and therefore individuals were far more likely to be aware if there were others about.

Other possible explanations are more bizarre. One that has been offered as to the appearance of mysterious footprints in the snow goes as follows. James Alan Rennie took photos of such tracks near Cromdale in Speyside in 1952: they were about 19 inches long, 14 inches wide, and were spaced about seven feet apart. There was no discernible difference between right and left foot, and they proceeded roughly in a single line. Rennie was able to offer an explanation for these prints because, some 30 years before in Northern Canada, he had witnessed some like them in the process of being made. He had watched the steps of a seemingly invisible giant approaching across pristine snow, and, as he recorded in his book *Romantic Speyside*, coming directly towards him:

'I stood stock-still filled with reasonless panic. The tracks were being made within fifty yards of me—20—10—then smack! I shouted aloud as a large blob of water struck me full in the face. I swung round brushing the water from my eyes, and saw the tracks continuing across the lake.

'In that moment I knew that the Wendygo, Abominable Snowman, Bodach Mór, or what have you, was for ever explained as far as I was concerned.'

Rennie reckoned that this phenomenon was caused by a freak warm air current travelling across much colder air, creating heavy concentrations of condensation which fell to earth as blobs of water. Certainly something like this seems to have been the cause of the prints he actually witnessed being created in Canada, but it does not follow that all prints are made in this way. There are, indeed, casts of Bigfoot's prints which are much more suggestive of an unknown animal's prints than of simple deposits of water.

Another explanation is that mountains are themselves

spiritual places, where supernatural events may occur in any case. Some Buddhists hold that Ben MacDui is home to one of the Bodhisattva or perfected beings who haunt the Earth and observe its creatures fulfilling their destinies. In this case, there is no need to be afraid of the Big Grey Man, for he has had hundreds and hundreds of lives and offers only help and comfort to human beings. Whether one takes the Buddhist view or not, however, there is much to be commended in the idea that the high places of the world, with the energies that may be stored in their solid masses of rock, may contain secrets and be capable of producing sights and sounds of which we have, as yet, no scientific understanding.

Affleck Gray, a noted writer who knows the Cairngorms intimately, has put together the most comprehensive account of possible explanations in his book *The Big Grey Man of Ben MacDhui* [sic]. He concludes by calling for future experiences to be subjected to rigorous examination. As the Cairngorms are no longer the lonely places they were fifty years ago, but are used recreationally by thousands, he says that the Big Grey Man may migrate to a less disturbed region, but that if he persists in manifesting himself, perhaps one day the physical properties of the mountain may be examined in conjunction with the psychic aspect; and that 'in the light of further research, the digging out of new facts, and the review of old ones in a new perspective, a reappraisal of the Grey Man phenomenon may be presented.'

In the meantime, we are left pondering the response given

to the travel writer Alistair Borthwick, when, after a day on Ben MacDui with a party of gamekeepers and stalkers, men who knew the mountains in all seasons and all weathers, he asked them if they thought there was any truth in the stories about the Big Grey Man. They looked at him for a few seconds, and then one said: 'We do not talk about that.'

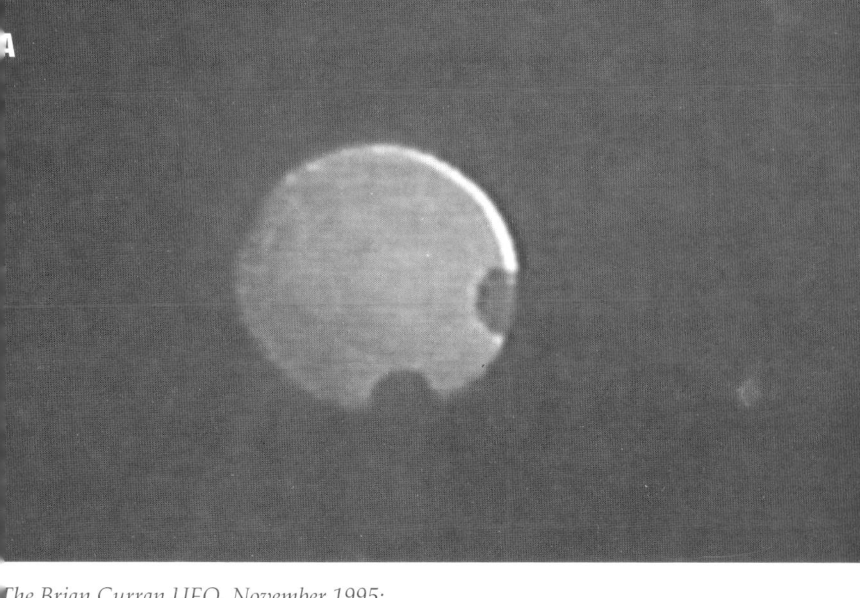

The Brian Curran UFO, November 1995:
A) The bright orange disc, with two missing sections
B) The disc moving away from the camera—the two semi-circular gaps have now been filled
C) The disc glowing intensely as it moves away at speed

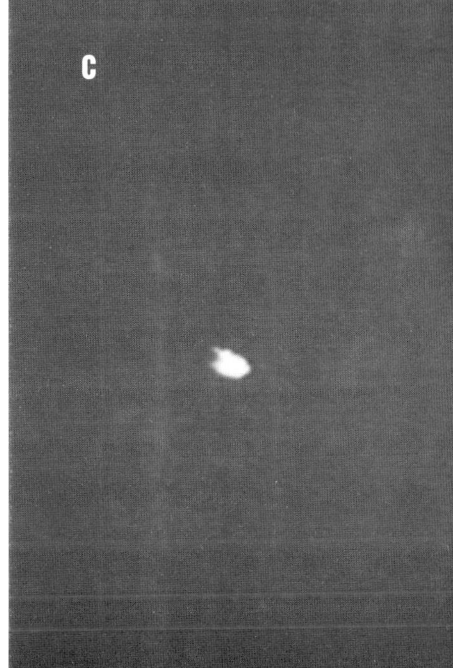

above:
Bob Taylor at the site of his close encounter in Dechmont Woods

right:
Bob Taylor identifying the tracks made by the spherical objects which emerged from the UFO

A

The Alec Bell UFO, November 1996:
(A) The white, glowing UFO as it appeared in the skies over Fauldhouse
(B) The object moving closer, with the missing sections of its rim remarkably similar to those of the UFO seen on the Curran video
(C) Now clearly visible as a white disc-shaped UFO with a raised rim, again similar to the Curran UFO

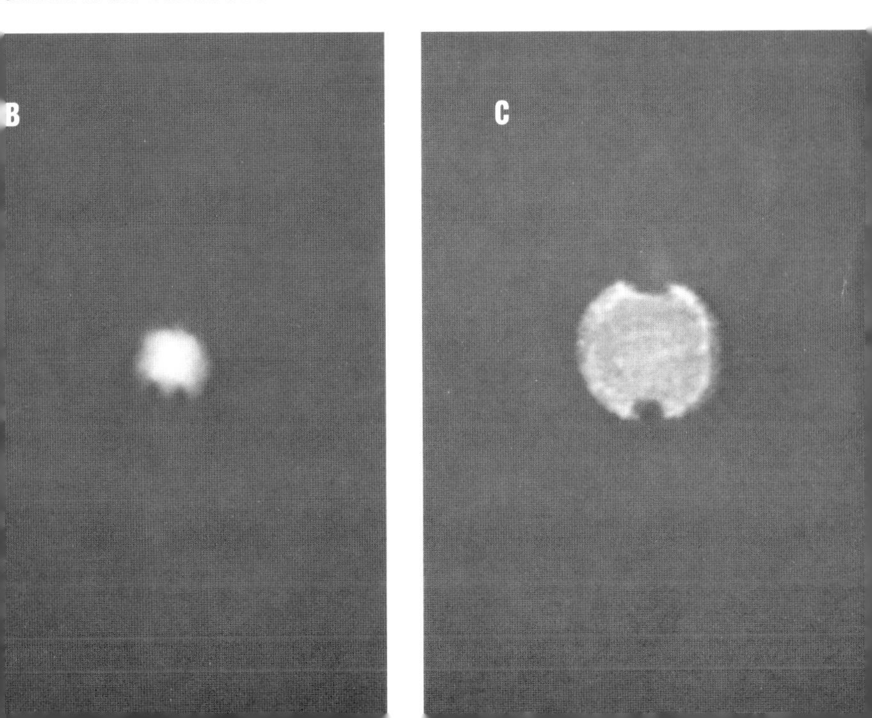

America's B2 Stealth Bomber
—have secret aircraft like this been tested at Scotland's Area 51?

The F117A Stealth Fighter
—a possible explanation for sightings of triangular UFOs

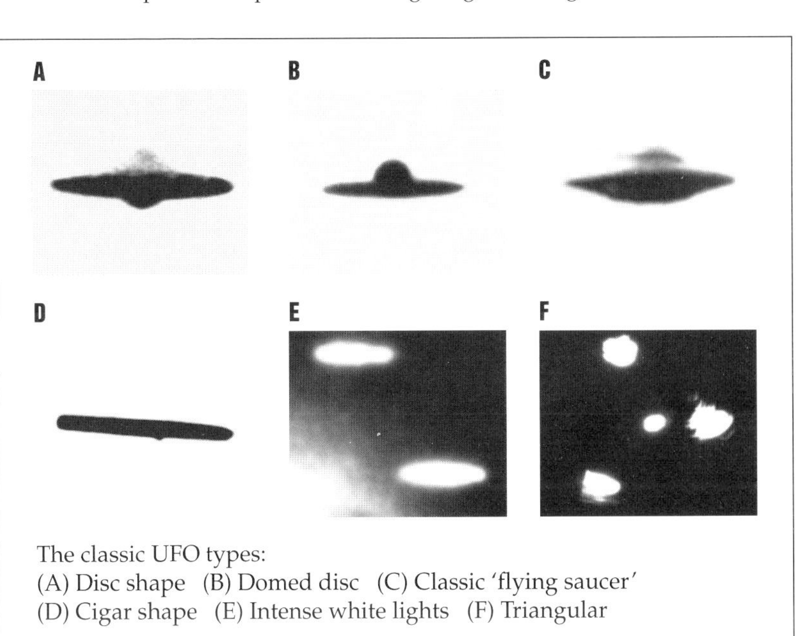

The classic UFO types:
(A) Disc shape (B) Domed disc (C) Classic 'flying saucer'
(D) Cigar shape (E) Intense white lights (F) Triangular

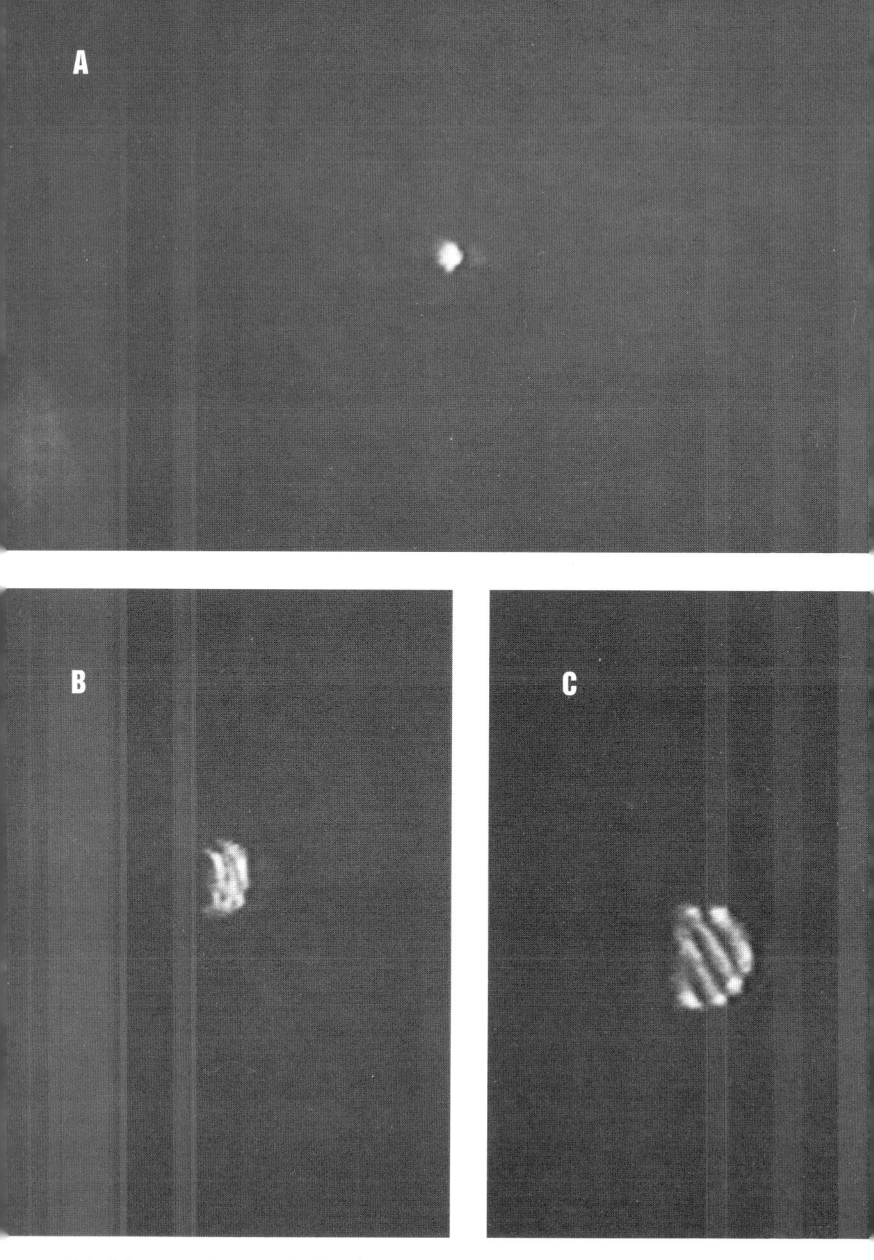

The Margaret Ross UFO, October 1996:
(A) The initial sighting of a bright, white light in the early morning sky
(B) The object beginning to transform itself, with bright bars of light emerging
(C) The final appearance of the object—half-moon shaped, with glowing diagonal bars across its surface

The crop circle at Corpach, August 1995

The lighthouse at Flannan Isle
—what fate befell the three men who vanished without trace in 1901?

above:
The Duke of Kent (*centre left*) —killed in an air crash in 1942 which has never been fully explained

left:
Willie McRae —his death in 1985 remains shrouded in mystery

Ben Alder: Who was the unknown man whose body was discovered near the summit on 22nd June 1996?

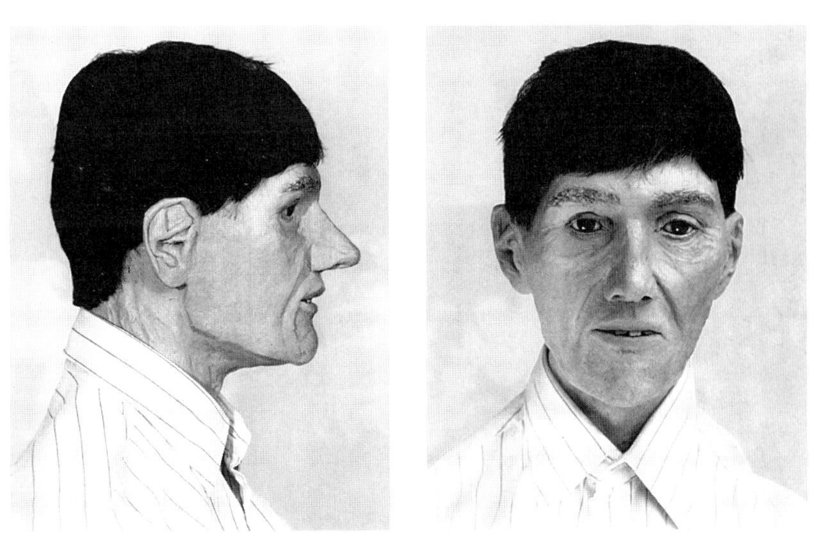

The reconstruction of the Ben Alder man, carried out by Di Cullington, an expert in craniofacial identification

The Fairy Knowe, near Aberfoyle

Glamis Castle—rumours persist about its terrible secret

above:
Callanish, on the Isle of Lewis—were stone circles used to contact distant civilisations?

right:
The Ring of Brodgar in Orkney—a UFO was seen here in 1994

Boleskine House—home of 'The Beast', Aleister Crowley (*inset*), and scene of bizarre occult rituals

```
FILE NO: ...................................... 018
SUBJECT: .........................highway apparitions
LOCATION: ......................throughout Scotland
DATE: ................................ 20th century
CLASSIFICATION: ............................... AN3
STATUS: ...................................... open
```

GHOST ROADS

Many roads in Scotland are haunted, apparently, by mysteriously appearing and vanishing vehicles. One of the most famous is in Skye—the A863 around Sligachan. Drivers and their passengers at night would become aware of a car's lights heading towards them, and often pulled into passing places, or proceeded cautiously round blind corners, expecting to come on a vehicle travelling in the opposite direction. But no such vehicle was seen, nor is there any track or side-road on to which it could have turned.

A similar experience used to be quite common on the mainland, on the A87 between Invergarry and Kyle of Lochalsh [the same road beside which Willie McRae died—*see File No. 031*]. Until about 1950, both at night and in daytime, a car would be seen approaching in the distance, but it would disappear inexplicably as it entered a bend in the road. But since the road was widened and modernised these sightings have diminished.

Again, on the A7 near Stow in the Borders, in the 1950s a phantom car was sometimes seen, and indeed it was the cause of several accidents. Drivers would follow behind a car for some time, and then suddenly find themselves going off the road into a ditch or even hitting a wall. The car ahead of them carried straight on, journeying down an old stretch of road which no longer existed. A similar manifestation occurs in Benbecula in the Outer Hebrides.

In East Lothian, a phantom bus is said to run on the B-road between Cockenzie and Prestonpans, but its seats are always empty. On the Hillfoots road between Dollar and Stirling, at Tait's Tomb (the burial place of Archibald Campbell Tait, a Victorian who, though born into a local Presbyterian family, became an Anglican priest and rose to become Archbishop of Canterbury), there is a bus-stop with an unusual reputation. Among many local stories circulating in the 1960s, one concerns a bus which was on the last run of the night back to Stirling, and was empty except for the driver and conductor. It pulled in at Tait's Tomb for a woman waiting at the stop. She went upstairs, and after a minute the conductor followed to take her fare. There was nobody there.

In November 1977, at Swinton in Berwickshire, a driver got a terrible shock when a large figure in a cloak and hood seemed suddenly to appear in the middle of the road. The driver braked as hard as he could, but was convinced that he had hit the pedestrian. He jumped out and ran to the front of the car, expecting to find a body underneath it. But there was no-one there, and no sign of any damage to the car.

In 1912, the first fatal road accident in Scotland took place on the road running through the Clyde Valley from Lanark to Hamilton, at Kirkfieldbank. Just at the entrance to Linnmill, which was then a fruit farm owned by the grandparents of the playwright and story-writer Robert McLellan, Robert's sister was knocked down and killed by a car. For years the sound of a car door being slammed shut has been heard by the inhabitants of Linnmill. There have been several different families living there, and all have heard the strange noise. On investigation, there is never any sign of a car, but the sound of the door being shut is, it is said, impossible to mistake.

```
FILE NO: ..................................... 019
SUBJECT: ................................ ley-lines
LOCATION: .....................throughout Scotland
DATE: ........................... 1920s to present
CLASSIFICATION: ............................. AN2
STATUS: .................................... open
```

STRANGE ENERGY BENEATH US

Scotland is reputed to be criss-crossed by ancient ley-lines. Dowsers, using wood or metal rods normally associated with water-divining, have reported encountering these strange forces. Ley-lines are thought of as the lines of a force field, perhaps only metres wide, which can run for long distances, apparently linking key historic sites—churches, castles, and stone circles. Intriguingly, however, they are also found running through modern buildings.

The mysterious phenomenon of ley-lines was first investigated in the 1920s by Alfred Watkins, an amateur archeologist, who made the startling discovery that many prehistoric monuments seemed to be arranged in straight lines, so that a ruler placed on a map would run through several such sites. Watkins concluded that leys were simply ancient trading routes, connecting various sites in the most direct way—rather like Roman roads, following a straight path whatever the obstacle. The problem with this theory is that the sites linked by leys ranged from neolithic stone circles to medieval castles—buildings constructed many centuries apart. But if ley-lines were not some sort of early roadway, what use did our ancestors make of them?

One of the most extraordinary examples of the power of ley-lines in Scotland came to light in the early 1990s at Craigpark school in Ayr, where staff and pupils were continually falling ill. There was no obvious reason why this should happen. The school, for pupils with learning difficulties, was only a few years old and had been purpose-built. Thousands of pounds of public money was spent in an effort to discover the source of the problem, yet at the end of this expensive exercise the experts were still baffled. The school was closed down, apparently a victim of 'sick building syndrome'. It was only later, through the activities of dowsers, that an answer was to be found—the school had been built at the intersection of a number of powerful ley-lines.

Craigpark was not a large building, about twice the size of a bungalow, but it had been inadvertently located right on an 'energy node'—a place where several leys crossed. The result was that the school was turned into a kind of bizarre psychic oven. The energy given off could not be seen, but, just as a radio receiver can pick up invisible radio waves, the human body all too readily registers the effect of ley energy. The result was a typical example of 'sick building syndrome'—

running noses, headaches, coughs and irritability—persistent problems which repeated trips to the doctor did not cure, because as soon as people returned to the building the symptoms would start up again.

It was suggested that the only way to cure the problem was to demolish the building, as the deflection of ley energy is not an exact science. Leys can be 'earthed' by digging metal tubes into the ground, or by placing stones at appropriate points around the affected site. These might have prevented the energy flowing through the building, but no-one knew if this might simply move the problem elsewhere.

Thousands of years ago this situation would not have occurred. Our ancestors were far more in tune with the landscape and instinctively knew where to place their buildings. Stone circles, those enigmatic monuments to prehistoric man which are still to be seen throughout the Scottish landscape, are thought to have been located to take full advantage of leys [*see File No. 023*]. It is no coincidence that wherever you find a stone circle you also experience a powerful aura. At these sites, straight lines of energy seem to become turned and twisted to form whorls and spirals. This may be a natural effect and could be the main reason why stone circles were located at these points. It may also be that the circles themselves act as some kind of conductor which affects the way this energy is channelled. If that is the case, what did our ancestors do with this energy?

Ley energy could have had both a practical and a mystical use. It may be that our prehistoric ancestors tried to control or expand the flow of energy to produce more crops. Or perhaps they tried to encourage leys to flow through their villages to produce harmony and a sense of well-being. But did they have an even more extraordinary purpose? One suggestion is that leys, if properly handled, can act as a door into another dimension or to other worlds. Did our forebears, through long-forgotten methods, use ley energy to allow spirits or other entities entry into our world? Or did they use it themselves as pathways into other worlds?

It has also been argued that stone circles were erected for some sort of astronomical purpose. The complex arrangements of stones at Callanish on the Isle of Lewis, for example, were clearly intended to align with stars, planets and the sun. The stones seem to have been used to plot the movement of a variety of heavenly bodies. But for what reason? Religious perhaps. Sun and Moon worship were common among pre-Christian peoples. Or was it simply a means of keeping track of the changing seasons? It has even been suggested that ancient peoples used these strange circles of power to contact distant civilisations. There are many tribes whose traditions include tales of their origins on distant planets. Some Yemen Arab sects, for example, believe that their race originated from the planet Mars, while the Dogon tribe of Africa are convinced that their ancestors came from a planet orbiting Sirius. Did the harnessing of ley energy allow some form of communication? We are so used to the idea of metal boxes and complex wiring systems that we have difficulty envisaging other ways of sending information. Yet we know that some people are able to carry out remote viewing, seeing things at a distance simply by making use of the hidden powers of the mind. Did our ancestors somehow use the energy patterns around stone circles to allow their own psychics to communicate over long distances?

It may well be that our ancestors' beliefs have had a longer-lasting effect than we realise. Edinburgh has a number of energy lines running through it, and perhaps this influenced its choice as Scotland's capital. For example, a typical ley runs from Arthur's Seat, through two churches on Edinburgh's south side, cuts along the wall of Edinburgh Castle, bisects the crossroads at the city's West End where Queensferry Road meets Princes Street, passes through Dean cemetery and terminates at Blackhall Church. A variety of buildings from different ages have been situated on the ley, some of which may well have been deliberately sited there to tap into the energy flow.

The ley effect is clearly present in many towns and cities throughout Scotland. It is believed, for example, that leys in Glasgow form a star shape, with the cathedral at the centre. Local investigator David Cown has suggested that the town of Crieff was, in the distant past, developed around a series of intersecting leys to form the shape of the star of David.

Although far better known to our ancestors, it seems clear that ley energy still affects our lives. What amazing powers might be revealed if we could unlock the hidden secrets which died with our ancestors?

FILE NO: 020
SUBJECT: ....the Brahan Seer
LOCATION: .... Easter Ross
DATE: ....16th/17th century
CLASSIFICATION: .... n/a
STATUS: .... open

'THE BLACK RAIN WILL EAT ALL THINGS'

The phenomenon of second sight has long been closely associated with the Scottish Highlands. Visions, dreams and predictions of the future based on, or related to, the 'gift' are common both in folk history, local tradition, and in contemporary Highland life. The most famous seer of all was Coinneach Odhar (*anglicé* Kenneth Or), most commonly known as the Brahan Seer. Ironically, although many people place great faith in the set of prophecies which have been handed down and are supposed to have been made by him, he remains a figure of mystery and confusion, about whom there is much uncertainty. It may even be that the Coinneach Odhar of legend is just that—a legend—conflated out of two distinct and different men who lived at least a century apart.

The prophecies are so well-known that they have become part of Scottish folk and literary heritage. In this, they resemble other predictions made by even older seers or wizards, such as Thomas the Rhymer and Michael Scott in the Borders. A comprehensive account of Coinneach's life and reputation, including many of his prophecies, was published in book form in 1877 by Alexander Mackenzie, the son of a crofter from Gairloch who had settled in Inverness and become a draper and an enthusiastic folklorist and clan historian. It was Mackenzie who designated Coinneach 'the Brahan Seer' (after Brahan in Easter Ross, where he was supposed to have lived). That Mackenzie had hit on a vein of popular interest was evident from the instant success of the book. It went through a number of editions, and, according to Highland historian Elizabeth Sutherland, until a new edition was published in 1970 'there were never less than fifty people on the waiting list at Inverness Library'. In total the book has now been reprinted more than 20 times and continues to sell all over the world.

Some of the most famous prophecies are as follows:

The day will come when a king will be born but never crowned.
Be sure there will be troublesome times at hand.

Known in Skye in 1918, this prophecy might refer to Edward VIII, who abdicated in 1936 before his coronation, just as the Spanish Civil War and the rise of tensions leading to the Second World War were taking place.

Sheep shall eat men, men will eat sheep, the black rain will eat all things. In the end old men shall return from new lands.

One of several prophecies referring to the Highland Clearances, and the introduction of the Cheviot sheep throughout the land. Other versions refer to 'the big sheep': the Cheviot was certainly a much bigger beast than the small, hardy Highland sheep it replaced. The 'black rain' has been variously interpreted. Some think it refers in some way to oil, either from the North Sea or perhaps from the Atlantic: exploration to the north and west of Scotland is now intense, and some predict a calamity of some kind if large-scale extraction begins, possibly in the form of a tanker accident in the Minch. Others suggest 'black rain' refers to nuclear fallout (such as occurred after the Chernobyl accident), and might be connected to the nuclear plant at Dounreay in Caithness. A third explanation is that it means acid rain. But in Gaelic the term 'black flood' or 'black rain' can simply mean a downpour, which might refer to any year or to any heavy flood, past, present or future.

However unlikely it may now appear, the Island of Lewis will be laid waste by a destructive war. . . . The Lewis then will enjoy a long period of repose.

This is a shortened version of a longer prophecy. Another Lewis prediction, of obscure origin, is that the island will be destroyed by sinking under the sea, and that the only survivors would be a woman with red shoes and three nuns. As recently as August 1997 a report in *The Scotsman* headlined this prediction in an article on scientific forecasts by Stuart Angus, a Lewis-born ecologist and government adviser for Scottish Natural Heritage. Angus revealed that the entire chain of Outer Hebridean islands from Lewis to Barra was sinking twice as fast as the British mainland, at a rate of 4.5mm per year. At this rate the highest hill in Lewis and Harris, the 800m Clisham, would disappear in 170,000 years. However, much of the Uists in particular is very low-lying, so that extensive flooding in coming decades is a distinct possibility. On the other hand, there is a possible connection with the next prophecy.

When the Ullapool ferry crosses to Stornoway,
it will sink with all lives lost.

According to Elizabeth Sutherland, in her book *Ravens and Black Rain*, this prophecy was in circulation in 1982. In 1995 a new £16 million ferry was built for this route, and was named *Isle of Lewis*. Some individuals are understood to be less than enthusiastic about making the trip aboard this vessel.

When a road runs up Eaval the second clearance will come
and the island will be populated by green men and grey geese.

Eaval is a 347m hill on North Uist. Although quite isolated, it is not impossible to imagine it topped with a radar or other mast, as many other summits of the Hebrides are. This would of course require a road or track for access. The 'green men' are thought to refer to soldiers: there is a large military presence at the missile range in Benbecula. Greylag and other geese winter in many of the islands, and indeed are protected now to such an extent that some schemes pay crofters compensation for the damage they cause to crops. A related prophecy says: *The day will come when the islands will be full of bent grass and big grey geese.*

Another prophecy reported to Elizabeth Sutherland spoke of a 'one-legged monster' which would leave Loch Kishorn and go twice below the water 'breathing fire'. The third time would spell disaster in the German ocean. The Ninian Central Platform built at Kishorn was a monolithic structure (not the usual four-legged kind), which was sunk twice before its final positioning. The flare stack, of course, 'breathes fire'.

> *The natural arch, or* Clach tholl, *near Storhead in Assynt will fall with a crash so loud as to cause the Laird of Leadmore's cattle, 20 miles away, to break their tethers.*

Hugh Miller, in his *Scenes and Legends of the North of Scotland* (1835), recorded that this was fulfilled when some of the laird of Ledmore's cattle were grazing on the lands of another proprietor. According to some, they were so startled by the noise of the arch when it fell, that they ran home in a panic, trampling anything in their path. A glance at the map, however, shows how unlikely this is.

Other prophecies relate to impending accidents and disasters. In Brora, Golspie and elsewhere on the east coast of Sutherland, one proposed that the bridge over the railway at Dunrobin station would collapse and kill the Duke of Sutherland. It is not explained how the 16th or 17th-century seer would have described this bridge, which of course in his day did not exist. But the fifth Duke seems to have known of the tale. He always alighted at the main station at Golspie and drove to Dunrobin Castle from there.

More interesting is the prophecy, remembered by Professor T. L. Marr of Emory University, Atlanta, *The day will come when a war will end at Loch Eriboll.* It was to the deep waters of Loch Eriboll that German U-boats came to surrender in May 1945.

The famous prophecy of Inverness, that 'full-rigged ships will be seen sailing eastward and west by the back of Tomnahurich Hill', was fulfilled by the construction of the Caledonian Canal in 1822. *The day will come when Tomnahurich will be under lock and key, with spirits secured within,* came true when the fairy hill in Inverness became a public cemetery, fenced and secured by a locked gate. The Seer also predicted piped gas and water in the town ('fire and water shall run in streams through the streets'), while the number of bridges crossing the Ness (five, seven or nine, depending on one's counting procedure) has been the subject of numerous prophecies. Local citizens still warn of catastrophes if the appropriate number is reached or exceeded.

The Seer also predicted the battle of Culloden, floods, bridge collapses, the fashionable spa town of Strathpeffer, and many other things. But who was he? Historically he may have been one of a number of warlocks, wizards, witches and others (numbering 6 men and 26 women) arrested in the Black Isle and surrounding area in 1577 and charged with diabolism and sorcery: the name Keanoch Ower appears in the list. If so, he was probably burnt, although there is no record of this. Elizabeth Sutherland, after extensive research, has proposed that he was a gypsy sorcerer or fortune-teller. Certainly this character is quite distinct from the more famous Coinneach Odhar of legend, who was believed to exist in the 17th century and whose most famous prediction was the extinction of the house of Seaforth. The earliest literary references to him do not occur until the second half of the 18th century.

According to these and later sources, he came from Uig in Lewis, but settled in Easter Ross at Brahan. His reputation as a seer was widespread: he apparently used a stone to 'see' into the future with. He acquired a certain notoriety for the frequency with which he foretold the destruction of various lairds, especially the powerful Mackenzies, who dominated the Ross-shire countryside. After some years making many of the predictions given above, he was summoned by Lady Isabella Seaforth to Brahan Castle. Her husband, the Earl, was on a diplomatic mission to France on behalf of Charles II, and had been away for some considerable time. Lady Seaforth wanted Coinneach to tell her what he could see of her husband, and what he was up to. He looked through his stone and told her that he was well and happy. She inquired more closely, but he would not elaborate, except to say that Seaforth was far too busy to think of returning from Paris. But the lady would not let it be, and insisted on knowing more. Eventually, during her birthday celebrations, she commanded him to tell her exactly what the Earl was up to. Coinneach was obliged to reveal that Seaforth had entirely forgotten about her and their children, as he was in love with a beautiful lady in Paris. He had no thought of coming home. Incensed at what she had probably suspected all along, and mortified that Coinneach had humiliated her in front of her guests, she decided to punish him for his insolence and for making ill use of an evil power. He would, she said, be put to death.

At this point, Coinneach delivered his famous prophecy, known as the Doom of the Seaforths:

> *I see into the far future, and I read the doom of the race of my oppressor. The long-descended line of Seaforth will, ere many generations have passed, end in extinction and sorrow. I see a chief, the last of his house, both deaf and dumb. He will be the father of four fair sons, all of whom he will follow to the tomb. He will live careworn and die mourning, knowing that the honours of his line are to be extinguished for ever, and that no future chief of the Mackenzies shall bear rule at Brahan or in Kintail. After lamenting over the last and most promising of his sons, he himself shall sink into the grave, and the remnant of his*

possessions shall be inherited by a white-coifed (or white-hooded) lassie from the East, and she is to kill her sister. And as a sign by which it may be known that these things are coming to pass, there shall be four great lairds in the days of the last deaf and dumb Seaforth—Gairloch, Chisholm, Grant and Raasay—of whom one shall be buck-toothed, another hare-lipped, another half-witted, and the fourth a stammerer. Chiefs distinguished by these personal marks shall be the allies and neighbours of the last Seaforth; and when he looks around him and sees them, he may know that his sons are doomed to death, that his broad lands shall pass away to the stranger, and that his race shall come to a end.

Having stunned his audience with this declaration, Coinneach was led away to execution. Seeing that there was no chance of escape, the story goes that he flung his seeing stone into the waters of Loch Ussie, saying that whoever found it would inherit his gift. Or, as told by Alexander Mackenzie, he threw the stone into a cow's hoofmark which was filled with water, saying that it would be found by a child born with two navels, who would discover the stone inside the belly of a pike, and would then have the second sight. A search was immediately made in the mud, 'when, lo! it was found that more water was copiously oozing from the boggy ground around, and rapidly forming a considerable lake, that effectually concealed the much-coveted stone. The waters steadily increased, and the result . . . was the formation of Loch Ussie.' Mackenzie claimed that he had been told that a man with two navels was born in the neighbourhood, and indeed was still alive in 1877.

Coinneach was reputedly burnt alive somewhere on Chanonry Point, head down in a barrel of pitch studded with many spikes. The site is not known, but in 1969 a stone memorial to the Seer was erected at Chanonry Point. It is, however, a monument to legend rather than to fact, as there is no historical proof that any of this took place. Indeed, the absence of any record, whether public or private, of such an event would imply the very opposite. The prophecy, however, in all its amazing detail, was widely known at the turn of the 18th and 19th centuries, before it was fulfilled in the following way.

The Earldom of Seaforth had expired after the 1715 Jacobite Rising, but the lands confiscated then were afterwards restored to the family. In 1794 the man who would be the last Mackenzie of Kintail (though not the last Lord Seaforth) came into his inheritance. He was Francis Humberston Mackenzie, born in 1755. As a boy at Eton, aged about 16, he became deaf after an attack of scarlet fever. This obviously had an effect on how much and how often he spoke, but it was not until the last two years of his life that he became unable, or unwilling, to speak at all.

He had four sons and six daughters; and although this must have augured well for the future of the line, he must have had some misgivings when he observed that four Highland lairds had the distinguishing marks of the prophecy. (It is not clear who these lairds were, although Elizabeth Grant of Rothiemurchus, in her *Memoirs of a Highland Lady*, identified one who was buck-toothed one and another who was mad.) And indeed, one by one his sons passed away: the first and second, William and George, died as children. Francis, the fourth, grew up and entered the Navy, but died a young man in 1813. Finally, the third son, William, who was MP for Ross-shire and generally reckoned to be 'the best and most able', died after a long illness. In 1815, Lord Seaforth, deaf and no longer speaking, also died.

The male line was now extinguished. The estates passed to his eldest daughter, Mary Frederica Elizabeth, who was married to, and therefore bore the surname of, Admiral Sir Samuel Hood, who was stationed in the East Indies, where his wife went with him. Sir Samuel died shortly before Lord Seaforth, so that Mary returned to inherit the estates in widow's weeds, that is hooded, and a Hood by name, from the East. She later remarried, but much of the land was sold off in the following years. In 1823, while driving her younger sister Caroline in a pony carriage in woods near Brahan, the ponies bolted and both women were thrown from the carriage. Mary was only bruised and shaken, but Caroline's injuries, after a long illness, proved fatal. Thus the line 'and she is to kill her sister' might be said to be fulfilled.

Francis Humberston Mackenzie was not, as has been mentioned, the last Lord Seaforth. His great-grandson, James Stewart-Mackenzie, was made Baron Seaforth of Brahan, but died in 1923 without a male heir. Brahan then passed to a great-nephew, but both he and his brother were killed in the Second World War, within 24 hours of each other, at Salerno. Brahan Castle was then inherited by a female cousin, but the building was in such disrepair that it was demolished. Since then the Seaforth lands continued to diminish. The 14,000-acre Kintail estate is now owned by the National Trust for Scotland. It has taken a long time, but the 'doom of the Seaforths', known by such as Sir Walter Scott *before* all its main features were fulfilled, is the most compellingly accurate prediction to be associated with the name of Coinneach Odhar, the Brahan Seer.

The best and fullest accounts of the Brahan Seer are to be found in Alexander Mackenzie's *The Prophecies of the Brahan Seer*, edited by Elizabeth Sutherland (1977), and in Elizabeth Sutherland's *Ravens and Black Oil* (1985).

FILE NO: 021
SUBJECT: .... crop circles/cattle mutilation
LOCATION: ....throughout Scotland
DATE: ....June 1990 to present
CLASSIFICATION: AN2
STATUS: ....under investigation

THE CROP CIRCLE PHENOMENON

Of all paranormal phenomena, crop circles appear to attract the greatest scepticism. Well-documented hoaxes are plentiful, and crop circle-making competitions have even been run by newspapers eager to heap ridicule on those who would investigate the origin of these strange creations.

Scotland too has had its share of hoaxes. In June 1991, near Prestwick, a crop circle was spotted from the air by a flying instructor. The 'circle' was in the shape of a fertility symbol, and a team of scientists was called in to investigate. Dr Nick Martin, of the Biochemical Sciences department of the Scottish Agricultural College at Auchincruive, was quoted in the local paper as saying that, though the team had not been able to reach a firm conclusion, 'If it is a hoax—and I doubt that—whoever has done it has the matter down to a fine art'.

The following week a group of students, calling themselves the 'British Gullible Society', admitted that they had created the circle—using nothing more complex than wooden planks and a rope. Needless to say, their admission caused embarrassment to the team of scientists, and considerable annoyance to some paranormal investigators, who failed to see the joke.

In contrast, the crop circle found in August 1995 at Corpach, near Fort William, is harder to dismiss. While almost all circles, including the Prestwick one, have been in fields of standing crops, the Corpach circle was in grass and reeds. Furthermore, it was not near any main road, and was only discovered by chance—in a location unlikely to have been chosen by hoaxers. Investigation of the site revealed no difference between the earth under the circle and that in the surrounding area, and there was no obvious natural—or man-made—cause.

Scotland's first confirmed crop circle appeared in June 1990 on the fringe of the town of Blairgowrie, in a field owned by the Ardblair estate bordering the A923. Unfortunately, the appearance of this phenomenon only came to the attention of Ron Halliday in late July, and by the time he arrived to inspect it the owner, Laurence Oliphant, had already harvested the field.

There had been, as it turned out, two circles. With the assistance of paranormal investigator Malcolm Robinson, and using dowsing techniques, Ron was able to locate the position of the circles and take measurements. At this late stage it was not possible, of course, to be exact: however, the upper circle was in the region of 70 feet in diameter, while the lower circle was only about half that size. Both circles had been formed at the western edge of the field beside a thick clump of trees which overhung the boundary of a disused stone quarry. The field itself covered almost the full slope of the hill on which it stood, and the formation had been created about one third of the way up.

Ron tested the site with dowsing rods and was surprised by the powerful response he experienced. It has been suggested that the existence of an unknown, yet 'natural', energy source might be a possible explanation of the circle phenomenon. However, it is not perhaps without significance that the first appearance of crop circles in Scotland should be near a town which witnessed one of the strangest UFO encounters ever recorded [*see File No. 005*].

The use of dowsing techniques at the site of a crop circle derives from the theory that there may be a link between ley energy and the formation of crop circles [*see File No. 019*]. It is known that ley energy can, in places, form whorl patterns, and it may be that this underground energy has an effect on crops growing above. The sudden appearance of crop circles would then be explicable as resulting from a transient build-up of ley energy which might subsequently dissipate or seek another path. On the other hand, non-varying ley concentrations could account for the fact that crop circles have on occasion been known to reappear in the same place.

Interestingly, it has been alleged that cattle died in mysterious circumstances in the same field close to the time that the Blairgowrie crop circles were formed. According to a witness (who does not wish to be identified) the necks of cattle in the field were found to have been broken, with no credible explanation as to how this could have occurred. So far, it has not been possible to confirm that this took place.

FILE NO: 022
SUBJECT: ....haunting of Ballechin House
LOCATION: ....nr. Logierait, Perthshire
DATE: 1877-1897
CLASSIFICATION: AN3
STATUS: .... closed

'IT WAS LIKE SUDDENLY ENTERING AN ICE-HOUSE'

Ballechin House stands two miles west of the village of Logierait in Perthshire. The incidents related here took place a hundred years ago, and bear no relation to the house as it stands today. But at the end of the 19th century Ballechin had, briefly, the reputation of being the most haunted house in Scotland. How this came about, and whether there was any foundation to the claim, can be judged by what follows.

The house was originally built in 1806, but by 1884 all but one still fairly substantial wing had been demolished. It was owned, until his death in 1877, by Major Robert Steuart, who by all accounts was an eccentric man, some said irascible and difficult. He seemed to take as much pleasure in the company of his dogs, of which he had many, as in that of humans. He believed in the idea of spirit return, and indeed often said that he would come back after death and enter the body of a particular black spaniel of which he was especially fond. So well-known were his statements on this matter that, after his death, all of his 14 dogs, including the spaniel in question, were shot, 'apparently in order to render impossible any such action on his part'. But in spite of this, the house soon acquired a local reputation for being haunted. People in the neighbourhood avoided its avenue after dark, and stories of strange apparitions and noises abounded.

The house had been inherited by a nephew of Major Steuart, but was generally rented out and looked after by a factor. In 1892 a Catholic priest named Father Hayden took a party of nuns on retreat there. He had been subjected, it was subsequently disclosed, to 'noises between his bed and the ceiling, like continuous explosions of petards, so that he could not hear himself speak . . .', and to other unusual experiences. In August 1896 the house was leased for a year to a wealthy family who intended to use it for shooting. They left after seven weeks. When, in an article in *The Times* the following year (which was written after visiting the house during an investigation into the haunting, as explained below) it was suggested that the disturbances which had caused the family to give up the lease were the result of mischief on the part of the tenant's children, the family's butler, one Harold Sanders, wrote to the paper to protest.

He had always been a sceptic as far as ghosts were concerned, he said, and even now remained one, but things that had happened at Ballechin had made him certain 'that there is something supernatural in the noises and things I heard and experienced. . . .' He described loud knockings which he at first thought came from the hot water pipes, but which could not be traced to that or any other 'mundane force'. Others had heard the same noises, and one man had had the feeling that someone was pulling the bedclothes off him at night. Sanders often sat up at night, to discover what was going on. 'When watching,' he wrote, 'I always experienced a peculiar sensation a few minutes before hearing any noise. I can only describe it as like suddenly entering an ice-house, and a feeling that someone was present and about to speak to me. On three different occasions I was awakened by my bedclothes being pulled off my feet.' Another night he heard groans and what sounded like 'someone being stabbed and then falling to the floor.' These noises almost always occurred at night, between about 2 and 4 a.m.

Before these and other anecdotes were made public in the newspapers, word of the house's reputation reached the Marquis of Bute, a member of the Society for Psychical Research. Through another member, Colonel Lemesurier Taylor, he arranged for a lease to be taken on Ballechin House, which had lain empty since the departure of the shooting tenants. A third member of the SPR, Miss Adela Goodrich-Freer, referred to in reports on the affair at the time as 'Miss X', was also involved. The idea was to carry out a full investigation into the alleged haunting. They invited a large number of guests to stay at Ballechin over a period of three months, from February to May 1897. The list included 11 ladies, 21 gentlemen, and the *Times* correspondent. When the article appeared in that newspaper on 8th June 1897, the house's owners were extremely annoyed that they had, as they thought, been duped into renting their property for such purposes. Lord Bute and Miss Freer totally refuted any idea of deception on their part, and indeed Miss Freer throughout the whole affair seems to have been remarkably immune to criticism of her attitude or methods. She it was who vetted the proposed list of guests and added to it, and it was she who suggested 'the keeping of a diary, in which everyone willing to do so should make entries, negative or affirmative.' Among those invited to visit was Frederick H. Myers, Honorary Secretary of the Society for Psychical Research and a leading figure in the then extremely fashionable investigation of the paranormal. To the forceful Miss Freer, Myers wrote (not perhaps without irony), 'If you don't get phenomena, probably no-one will.'

The *Times* correspondent, after the investigation was over, criticised the SPR for having in the past made 'many investigations in a perfunctory and absurd manner by sending somebody to a haunted house for a couple of nights and then writing an utterly worthless report.' For real continuity, he suggested, a couple of intelligent detectives should have been used over the whole period. Miss Freer, who organised the house party, was disadvantaged simply because she was a lady and therefore had her duties as a hostess to attend to, making her unfit to carry out the investigation properly.

'Some of her assistants sat up all night, with loaded guns, in a condition of abject fright; others, there is reason to suspect, manufactured phenomena for themselves; and nearly all seem to have begun by assuming supernatural interference, instead of leaving it for the final explanation of whatever might be clearly proved to be otherwise inexplicable.'

In their published account, *The Alleged Haunting of B— House* (1899), Freer and Bute repudiated these allegations—in particular the idea that anything at present imperfectly understood must therefore be 'supernatural'. They themselves, they stressed, believed that 'all things which exist, or can exist, are, *ipso facto*, natural, although their nature may not belong to the plane of being in which we are normally accustomed to move.' This was and is an admirable standpoint. Nevertheless, Freer from the outset seemed determined (as Frederick Myers had hinted) to discover phenomena at Ballechin, whether natural, supernatural or otherwise.

In an article on the investigation in *The Nineteenth Century* (August 1897), she explained how she went about it. 'Some of my friends asked me how I proposed to organise a haunted house research, to which I could only reply that I didn't propose to do anything of the sort. It seemed to me that among several things to be avoided was self-consciousness of any kind, that the natural thing to do was to settle down to a country-house life, make it as pleasant as possible, and await events. . . . The subject of the "haunting" was never accentuated, and we always tried to prevent talking it over with newcomers. . . . As to the guests, for the most part they came on no special principle of selection. . . . Several of our visitors had more or less special interest in the inquiry, but others merely came for a country-house visit or for sport, and some knew nothing whatever till after their arrival of any special interest alleged to attach to the house.' Note that 'till after their arrival'. Clearly, even those who came without ghost-hunting in mind were soon made aware that they should be on the look-out for strange phenomena.

A butler, cook, and two housemaids were first to arrive, to prepare the house. Miss Freer and her friend Miss Constance Moore came from Edinburgh, on 3rd February 1897, with their maid. There was snow on the ground, and although it was not cold outside, the house itself was gloomy and 'like a vault', having lain empty through the winter. No provisions had arrived as ordered. The two ladies made a supper of bread, milk and tinned meat bought in Logierait, and went to bed. 'The room,' the communal diary (in fact, nearly all of it would be compiled by Freer) recorded, 'was so cold that we had to cover our faces, and we had no bed-linen.'

At 3 a.m. on this their very first night they woke to 'a loud clanging sound . . . distinctly as of metal struck with wood; it seemed to come diagonally across the house.' This went on for two hours. At about 4.30 they heard voices, apparently in the maid's room above them. They then fell asleep again.

When the maid brought in tea at 8 a.m., she said that she had slept very badly, having been worried over the apparent restlessness of the ladies, as she had heard 'voices and footsteps and the sound of things dragged about' downstairs.

But none of either the ladies or the maids had got up in the night let alone gone downstairs.

That evening, Freer and Moore decided to take a stroll down the avenue, which the locals avoided after dark. On that occasion, and again the following evening, they noted that their dog Scamp, 'who never does bark except under strong excitement', barked and growled at the fir plantation beside the road.

The factor called, promised to put right a few problems with frozen pipes and such matters, and apologised for the 'havers' of a locally hired kitchenmaid, who had refused to spend a night in the house. The factor, Freer noted, seemed keen to '"keep out the natives" and their chatter.'

That night the maids heard sounds below them 'of continuous speaking or reading', and rather sensibly (though apparently incorrectly) 'supposed the young ladies were reading to one another'.

The house party grew in size. A Ouija board had been brought along, and was consulted about the name of a handsome woman whose portrait hung in the library. The word ISHBEL was given several times, as was MARGET. Freer explained that these were Gaelic pronunciations of the names Isobel and Margaret, and expounded on what this signified: 'It was obvious . . . that the intelligence from which the writing proceeded . . . could write in English, and was familiar with the colloquial Gaelic pronunciation of the name, but was unacquainted with the Gaelic orthography.'

The same evening, it was decided to explore what was

now referred to as 'Scamp's Copse' before dinner. Walking with a Mr L. F— and a Mr F—, within minutes Freer saw something remarkable. 'Against the snow I saw a slight black figure, a woman, moving slowly up the glen. She stopped, and turned and looked at me. She was dressed as a nun. Her face looked pale. I saw her hands in the folds of her habit. Then she moved on, as it seemed, on a slope too steep for walking. When she came under the tree [a large oak tree] she disappeared. . . .

'I described what I had seen. The others saw nothing. This did not surprise me, for though both have been for many years concerned in psychical investigation, and have had unusual opportunities, neither has ever had any "experience", so that one may conclude that they are not by temperament likely to experience either subjective phenomena or even thought-transference.'

The names given by the Ouija board were thought to refer to Isabella Margaret Steuart, sister of Major Steuart, who died in 1880, aged 66. She became a nun at the age of 35. Later, from the nunnery where she lived and died, Freer and Bute obtained a description of her which said (obviously in respect of specific questions asked), 'we do not know whether she could speak Gaelic. She was very fond of Scotland, and very particular about the pronunciation of Scotch names.'

Miss Freer would see the nun, whom she christened 'Ishbel', on several occasions in 'the Glen' or avenue. Sometimes she was with an older woman in grey. On 8th February, for example, she saw and heard them in earnest conversation together but could not make out the words. Others with her saw nothing but claimed to hear two women's voices.

Almost on a daily basis, one or more people at Ballechin were now hearing what were recorded as 'audile phenomena' in or around the house. A table of these sounds, printed in the 1899 account, contains 115 incidents, ranging from the loud clanging sound heard on the first night, to continuous reading, reverberating bangs, footsteps, 'noises percussive or explosive', voices in conversation, animal noises, 'footsteps of an old man shuffling in slippers', groans, heavy falls and thuds, loud rappings on doors, resounding crashes, explosions, violent hammerings and voices in argument. The sheer number of sounds is impressive, perhaps too impressive—although other cases of, say, poltergeist activity, do record large numbers and varieties of noises and actions. No fewer than 36 of the noises heard at Ballechin were witnessed by Miss Freer herself. 25 of them were witnessed by her friend Miss Moore, and when another lady friend, Miss Langton, arrived, she too demonstrated the temperament so lacking in Mr L. F— and Mr F— by witnessing 26 of them. Of all of these, Freer and Moore witnessed 18 audile phenomena together, while Freer and Langton witnessed 16 together. All three ladies together witnessed four of them. Whether a competitive element existed between Misses Moore and Langton cannot, of course, be proved from these statistics.

When nothing much was happening in the house in terms of phenomena (which was rarely), the party tried various experiments, including thought-transference and crystal-gazing, but 'nothing came of it in regard to the house.'

Then, on 16th February, Miss Freer had a new event to write about: 'I had an experience this morning which may have been purely subjective, but which should be recorded. About 10 a.m. I was writing in the library, face to light, back to fire. Mrs W— was in the room, and addressed me once or twice, but I was aware of not being responsive, as I was much occupied. I wrote on, and presently felt a distinct, but gentle, push against my chair. I thought it was the dog and looked down, but he was not there.' The same thing happened again. She even thought it was Mrs W—! But on looking round, the room was empty. Just then, Mrs W— returned. The dog was on the hearthrug, where she had expected him to be.

Freer saw the two ghostly women again in the Glen, 'Ishbel' on her knees 'in the attitude of weeping', 'Marget' apparently reasoning with her in a low voice.

The same night, Miss Langton had a dream of a strange figure in the corridor of Ballechin. As she described it, 'his face was quite distinct, and what struck me most was the curious way in which his hair grew on his temples. His eyes were very dark, keen, and deep-set; his face was pale, and with a drawn, haggard expression. He looked about thirty-nine years of age. His hair was dark and thick, and waved back from his forehead, where it was slightly grey. It was a most interesting and clever face, and one that would always, I should think, attract attention. He was dressed in a long black gown like a cassock, only with a short cape, barely reaching to the elbows.'

This, as Freer later explained, was the only occasion when a witness at Ballechin would see the 'phantasm' of someone still living. For on 25th May, Freer and Moore would meet, for the first time, in a crowded railway station, the Catholic priest Father Hayden who had been disturbed by loud explosions at Ballechin in 1892. Of the identity of the phantasm, the two ladies said, no doubt could be felt from Miss Langton's description. Ballechin was a place, Freer wrote, to which the priest's thoughts were 'naturally and disagreeably drawn' when he was asleep, and this accounted for his presence in Langton's dream. On awaking, she opined, he would probably have no recollection of being in the corridor, 'or at the utmost would have an impression of having dreamt that he was there.'

More guests arrived, and some departed. Some saw the nuns, others heard the bangs and voices. They all changed bedrooms frequently, to try out the so-called 'ghost rooms'. Some heard a sound like a man walking and a dog pattering beside him. Their own dogs seemed to sense and growl at invisible things. Rooms were locked and experiments carried out to try to discover where the various noises were coming from, and whether 'normal' sounds could carry through the building as some of the audile phenomena seemed able to do. There were also sightings of a 'brown cross'. When Freer, Moore and Langton went away for four nights to St Andrews, Langton indulged in a spot of crystal-gazing there, and recorded in her private journal that she distinctly saw, in one of the rooms at Ballechin ('No 3'), a tall woman, dressed in a long clinging robe of grey, who seemed to be holding something in her hand against the wall at the foot of the bed. 'This became more distinct, and I saw that it was a cross of dark brown wood, some 12 inches long (I should say).'

This was an extraordinary coincidence. Freer, stressing that Langton 'certainly' had not been informed that others had seen a brown cross (one wonders how she was so certain), explained it thus: 'For those not accustomed to the phenomenon of crystal-gazing, it may be as well to remark that it is quite possible that the image had been subconsciously seen by Miss Langton when sleeping in No 3, as deferred impressions are often externalised for the first time in the crystal. She may equally have received the impression by thought-transference from others.'

The investigation proceeded apace after their return to Ballechin. Violent bed-shaking, moving lights, limping or scuttering noises, explosions, bell-ringing and knocks at doors were all witnessed. Some of the maids were also seeing and hearing things and one was becoming hysterical. Freer wrote that she was very pleased by the arrival of a new guest, Mrs M—, because she was a Roman Catholic, and, 'according to previous evidence, so were other persons upon whom specially interesting phenomena had been bestowed.' Not surprisingly, on her first night, Mrs M— was awakened by a terrific noise, 'like the lid of a coal-scuttle having caught in a woman's gown'. Later she heard a distant cannon, 'exactly like the one o'clock gun in Edinburgh, and the whole morning a ceaseless chatter. . . .' Before the end of the investigation, more Catholics would be invited to Ballechin, including a bishop and several priests. This religious bias seems strange, to say the least, but the bishop said a mass and the priests prayers, and oddly enough, after these various acts were performed the apparitions ceased and the bangs diminished and then also ceased.

Before that, though, there was some evidence that the locals, who were well aware that there were a number of ladies and gentlemen carrying out research on the hauntings, might have been contributing to the show. On 6th April, Freer's diary entry reads: 'This afternoon Mrs S—, a lady well acquainted with the neighbourhood, came to tea. She asked me about the hauntings, and said they were matter of common talk in the district. She also told me that in the late Mr S—'s time it had been alleged that the disturbances were intentional annoyances, though she agreed it was rather a sustained effort.' Shortly before this visit, noises outside the house had been heard at night, as of a prowler on the gravel. Nobody had been caught, but the diary for 2nd April reads: 'An unpleasant light has (possibly) been thrown on these movements. We find today that someone has killed a sheep in the garden, in a retired spot, taking away the skin and the meat.'

On Thursday 8th April, Freer's diary noted that, though she, Miss Langton, and a Mr T— had planned to leave the day before (it was the Easter weekend, which they planned to spend elsewhere), she had realised that the 8th was the anniversary of Major Steuart's death, and that 'it would be a pity—on the hypothesis of there being anything supernormal in these phenomena—that the house should not be under observation tonight.' They particularly wanted to observe the downstairs smoking-room, which was known as 'the Major's room'. But Freer was suffering from a headache, and spent the afternoon lying down in her bedroom. In the evening, a few minutes before dinner, she went down to the Major's room and busied herself in putting her camera to rights.

'It was a delicate piece of work, and when I saw a black dog, which I supposed for the moment to be "Spooks" (my Pomeranian), run across the room towards my left, I stopped, fearing that she would shake the little table on which the camera stood. I immediately saw another dog, really Spooks this time, run towards it from my right, with her ears pricked. Miss Langton also observed this, and said, "What is Spooks after?" A piece of furniture prevented my seeing their meeting, and Spooks came back directly, wagging her tail. The other dog was larger than Spooks, though it also had long black hair, and might have been a small spaniel.'

'It was not till after we had left B—,' Freer wrote later, in a scarcely credible note, 'that we learned that the Major's favourite dog was a black spaniel.' But Miss Langton's private journal backed up Freer's account, as it did what happened later, when the two ladies and Mr T— were sitting round the fire in the smoking-room after dinner.

'Suddenly,' wrote Langton, 'one of us called out, "Listen to those footsteps," and then we *distinctly* heard a heavy man walking round the room, coming apparently from the direction of the safe, in the wall adjoining the billiard room, and then walking towards the door, passing between us and the fireplace in front of which we were sitting. It was a very curious sensation, for the steps came so very close, and yet we saw nothing.' The footsteps died away, but later they all heard the voices of a man and woman, raised as if in anger, arguing outside the door. This happened three times, but each time when they opened the door there was no-one to be seen.' Just before going to sleep at one o'clock, Langton again heard the sound of 'a heavy man in slippers come down the corridor and stop near my door, and then the sound of a long argument and subdued voices, a man and a woman.'

Frederick Myers visited Ballechin at Easter and was not impressed by the methods being employed in the investigation. In a letter to *The Times* in June, after the article on Ballechin had appeared, he would refute the suggestion that the Society for Psychical Research authorised any statements made about the alleged haunting there. 'I visited B— . . . before your correspondent's visit, and decided that there was no such evidence as could justify us in giving the results of the inquiry a place in our *Proceedings*.'

What is to be made of this extraordinarily long and detailed investigation? The sceptic is inclined to agree with Myers. There is evidence, from *before* the Freer-Bute investigation, that something weird was going on at Ballechin

House. (See the remarks of Father Hayden and Mr Sanders.) But the house-party that tried to see and hear ghostly or other phenomena there in early 1897 was so large, and made up of so many different people, many of whom arrived with prejudices and opinions which ought to have disqualified them at the outset, that the episode is more interesting as a social history text than as a serious effort to discover truths about alleged haunted places. Whatever mystery Ballechin may have contained, it was, we must conclude, effectively destroyed by the antics of Adela Goodrich-Freer and her guests.

FILE NO: 023
SUBJECT: .... standing stones
LOCATION: .... Isle of Lewis/Orkney
DATE: .... prehistoric/unknown
CLASSIFICATION: .... n/a
STATUS: .... open

SECRETS OF THE STONES

There are hundreds of standing stones and stone circles scattered the length and breadth of Scotland's mainland and islands, and of course many more throughout the British Isles. They vary hugely in size, shape and location, in the way they are positioned, whether singly or in groups, in whether they are marked, elaborately decorated or plain, and in many other ways. What is their significance? Are they the key to one or more cultures that preceded ours, now lost forever? Do they still hold important meaning for our understanding of the Earth and its relationship to other planets and stars? Are they even, as some have suggested, signs that Earth was visited in the past by aliens?

The theories developed to understand these prehistoric remnants are many and varied. In medieval times giants were held responsible for having erected the vast monuments. Later, when bones were discovered on the sites, the theory grew that the stone circles in particular were temples, used for human sacrifices. At Loanhead of Daviot in Aberdeenshire a central pit was found to contain fragments of burnt bone, belonging to a man aged about 40 years. Was this an elaborate cremation site for an important person. Or did the bones belong to a sacrificial victim? If so, who killed him? The Druids, that weird quasi-priestly sect, were often blamed for acts of sacrifice that may have taken place.

Then, in the 18th and 19th centuries, people studied the circles and stones more closely. Maes Howe in Orkney, for example, is a burial chamber, built 5,000 years ago. But the long low passage into it, pointing roughly in the direction of the sunset, is so constructed that, on the shortest days of the year, when the sun is low, its rays penetrate right into the chamber and strike the back wall. Why was it so important for the people who built the tomb that this should occur? And, equally interestingly, how did they manage to build it so accurately that this happened?

Most of the stones were erected somewhere between 3,000 and 5,000 years ago. The Hill o' Many Stanes at Mid Clyth, Caithness, consists of 22 rows of small, low-set stones, some 200 in number, which were once part of a fan-shaped pattern running north-south down the south-facing slope. 600 stones may originally have been in place. What were they for? Were they ghost-paths for sending the dead on their way, or along which they could be contacted? Or were they, more mundanely, markers within which clans or families met as if in primitive church pews? The huge Ring of Brodgar in Orkney once had as many as sixty stones in its circle. The diameter of this perfect circle is more than 100 metres, and it has been estimated that building it, together with its ditch cut into solid rock, would have taken 80,000 man-hours. Many people could have gathered within it for ceremonies. But at Callanish in Lewis, the inner circle is much smaller—perhaps only priests were allowed in it. Callanish has straight lines of stones running from this centre out to the four points of the compass, with the site lying on a north-south axis. How important were these directional lines? Other stones in the vicinity somehow seem connected, as though forming part of a pattern over the whole island landscape.

Is the tall central stone found at the centre of Callanish and other circles like the Stones of Stenness in Orkney the gnomon of a giant sundial? Were standing stones once a complex mapping system throughout the land, used to help travellers and others to know the topography when there were no roads or permanent settlements? Certainly the idea of a class of astronomer-priests gained great credence in the 19th century. More recently, people have investigated the connections between groups and individual stones, claiming that they are often connected by ley-lines, the straight human-made lines that criss-cross the landscape like a grid [*see File No. 019*]. And, as mentioned, some people have even suggested that the stones were airstrips or landing-pads for flying saucers visiting from space.

Most stones used in the construction of the circles came from nearby, but even so, some had to be transported, presumably dragged, over incredibly rough, boggy country before being erected in position. At Old Keig in Aberdeenshire, for example, one of the stone formations typical of the north-east which show an astronomical relation to the rising and setting of the moon in the southern sky, the massive 'recumbent' stone which is the centrepiece weighs around 60 tons and was brought from a source some 6 miles away. Furthermore, this gigantic slab was so meticulously placed, manoeuvred, adjusted, that even today its surface remains quite horizontal. These recumbent circles generally have two tall upright stones on either side of the recumbent block. In front of them, large numbers of fine white quartz fragments were scattered, which would have picked up the moon's light and reflected it. What did this signify? Were the quartz pieces seen as bits of the moon itself, or did they somehow represent some link to the moon, which was possibly seen as the place the dead went to, just as the sun was the place life came from?

Some stone formations have been badly affected over the centuries, by weather, by stones being removed for building, or by other developments. A quarry lies just below the hillside of Tomnaverie in Aberdeenshire, on top of which stands a recumbent stone circle and central cairn. Midmar Kirk in Aberdeenshire is now located within a churchyard. On the other hand, new stones are still being discovered. At Machrie Moor in Arran, for example, there are extensive and varied formations—some built of granite boulders, others of taller red sandstone pillars, some with a mixture of stone which brings out colour variations—including a low stone circle that had until the 1970s lain hidden for centuries under layers of peat. It may be impossible to discover, so far removed in time from those who built them, the purpose of all these circles, but we can be sure that the mysterious influence they exert on the countryside around them, and on those who visit them, will last long after our own time.

FILE NO: 024
SUBJECT: .... loch monsters
LOCATION: .... Highlands
DATE: .... AD 565 to present
CLASSIFICATION: AN3
STATUS: .... under investigation

CREATURES FROM THE PAST— OR BEYOND?

On 18th August 1990 Alistair McKellaig, accompanied by his brother Duncan and young sons Neil and Steven, was fishing on Loch Morar when he caught sight of three distinct humps moving in formation about 50 yards behind their boat. The object was keeping pace with them and he could clearly see the humps standing two or three feet out of the water, leaving a distinctive wake behind them. He and his companions could hardly believe what they were seeing, but after a short time the mystery creature overtook the boat, then submerged, leaving the loch as calm and clear as before. Alastair regularly fishes on the loch and is familiar with local conditions, but he knows he saw something that day which he is unable to explain.

This is by no means the only sighting of 'Morag'—as the Loch Morar monster has come to be known. Although less famous than Nessie, the total number and frequency of sightings is impressive. In 1969, for example, a sighting very similar to the McKellaigs', but altogether more frightening, was reported by William Simpson and Duncan McDonnell.

While cruising in their motorboat on the loch on August 16th, they noticed a loud splashing noise coming from behind the boat. Duncan looked up and saw an object rushing towards them, following in their wake. According to Duncan, 'It only took a matter of seconds to catch up on us'. The animal, in fact, hit the boat side on. He was certain that this was intentional. The collision brought the beast to a halt, but Duncan was by now thoroughly alarmed and grabbed an oar to protect them from a further attack. He was worried that it might go beneath the boat and try to capsize them. William Simpson had been below, but rushed on deck when he heard the commotion. He too saw the animal, which was about 25 to 30 feet long and with three humps protruding from the water. Its skin appeared to be rough and a dirty brown colour. A snake-like head was raised above the waves. Terrified by the sight, William grabbed his shotgun and fired in the direction of the creature. It showed no obvious ill-effects, but rapidly disappeared into the murky blackness of the loch.

At over 1,100 feet deep, Loch Morar is one of the deepest lochs in Europe. A few small islands huddle near the western shores close to Mallaig, but otherwise the eleven-mile-long loch is a forbidding place with steep cliffs plunging deep into the water. Perhaps it is the rugged isolation of this landscape which inspires the imagination, but there have been so many sightings here that the phenomenon is hard to ignore. In 1996, a diver brought some bones up from the loch floor, and many wondered if this could be the evidence of Morag they had been looking for. But scientific analysis soon revealed that this was, in fact, simply the skeleton of a deer. Although some have reported seeing mysterious footprints on the shoreline, and have speculated that Morag may have taken a deer while foraging on land, it would appear that on this occasion there was no contact with Morag, and it was simply a deer which had drowned in the loch.

Loch Morar is part of the acknowledged 'monster triangle' in Scotland, which also comprises Lochs Ness, Oich, Lochy, Quoich and Shiel. In this small area sightings of strange aquatic beasts have occurred with astonishing regularity. It has even been suggested that these stretches of water are connected by some subterranean system which allows a large unknown animal to move undetected from one loch to another, though in view of the lochs' differing levels this seems highly unlikely.

Historically, reports of strange loch monsters stretch far back into the mists of time. When St Columba visited the Highlands in AD 565, he reported a confrontation with a water beast on the River Ness, some way downstream from the loch, but it was not until this century, and in particular the case of schoolteacher Donaldina Mackay which hit the headlines in 1933, that the modern wave of Nessie reports began to appear.

Like Loch Morar, Loch Ness is a treacherous place, deep and unpredictable. The Great Glen in which Ness lies is notoriously susceptible to sudden weather changes. Wind rushes through it as if through a gigantic funnel, with dramatic effects on the surface of the loch. At one moment it can seem as calm as a millpond. The next it turns into a storm-lashed sea, with huge waves pounding up and down the loch. It is a treacherous place, even for those who know it well. The inviting shoreline drops sharply—walk in just a few feet and you find that you cannot touch the bottom. The water is cold, it rarely reaches 6°C even in summer, and below the surface the murky waters make it impossible to see clearly.

It was here that Donaldina Mackay described what she saw as 'an aquatic creature twelve to fifteen feet long with a rounded back', and this classic description of the Loch Ness monster has been repeated by numerous other witnesses in the years since. But no monster has ever been caught, and no conclusive evidence of its existence has so far come to light.

In June 1993 Edna McInnes and her boyfriend Douglas Mackay reported an extraordinary encounter with Loch Ness's mysterious occupant. Edna described seeing a 'giraffe-like head and neck' appearing out of the water as they headed towards the loch. After spotting Nessie, Edna drove at speed to her mother's house and from the beach at Dores the couple had a second sighting of the 'monster'. It had now come within 20 feet of the shore and its long neck could be clearly seen. It was light brown in colour and left a massive white trail behind it. It seemed to be swimming just below the surface, but they could follow its movements by the trail of bubbles which broke the surface of the water.

One witness who is most closely associated with the Loch Ness sightings is Alex Campbell, who claimed to have seen the animal no less than eighteen times. For many years he was the loch's water bailiff, employed by Ness Fisheries Board. It was through Mr Campbell that the Mackay sighting in 1933 came to public notice, but shortly after this Campbell, a controversial figure, claimed that he too had experienced a sighting. His description was similar to Donaldina Mackay's. According to an account at the time he 'saw a creature raise its head and body from the loch . . . a small head on a long neck . . . the creature seemed fully 30 feet in length'. Later, investigator Tim Dinsdale, notable for some remarkable film footage which he took of Nessie, showed a number of drawings to Mr Campbell, who was able to identify an illustration of a plesiosaurus—a dinosaur which has been extinct for millions of years—as being identical to the creature he had seen.

Stranger still, Loch Ness has been linked to UFO activity. Ted Owens, who claimed to have met extraterrestrials several times, reported that his alien visitors took him to the Loch-side where he saw the animal rise out of the water. He had no idea what the purpose of this demonstration was.

Next to Loch Morar, separated by a thin, hilly stretch of land, lies Loch Glenn. In June 1997 Hamish Smith was flying over the area with Father Michael Hudson, when they spotted a large blue and red object lying just below the loch's surface. Hamish reported that 'It was not a shoal of fish and the entrance to the loch is only eight metres deep so it couldn't be a submarine'. Hamish's drawing shows an object that would not look out of place in a USO* report. Divers who subsequently went down to take a look could not find anything that would account for Hamish's strange sighting.

Many have no doubt that these loch monsters are flesh and blood beasts. But if that is the case, why after so many sightings has not a single 'monster' been caught? Can it all be a hoax? Undoubtedly, there have been many well-documented hoaxes, but there have also been many apparently reliable sightings.

Another theory is that these are creatures from another dimension. There is no doubt that Loch Morar is criss-crossed with powerful ley-lines, and perhaps these energy currents allow us, at certain times, to see into another dimension, possibly even into the past. This might explain why Nessie and Morag are often seen, yet no concrete evidence of their existence is ever found. Perhaps we are not dealing with a flesh and blood beast, but a phantom—a ghost.

* The term USO—unidentified submersible object—has been coined as a result of the numerous reports that have emerged worldwide of strange craft which have the ability to venture underwater.

But whatever the truth, the secrets of the murky, unexplored depths of Loch Ness, Loch Morar and the others continue to defy all explanation.

FILE NO: 025
SUBJECT: .... nature spirits
LOCATION: .... throughout Scotland
DATE: .... ongoing
CLASSIFICATION: AN3
STATUS: .... open

THE HIDDEN WORLD

Ghosts, UFOs and poltergeists have become well established as areas of paranormal activity worthy of serious investigation. The same cannot be said of fairies. We seem ready to accept the idea of aliens visiting the Earth, but 'nature spirits', as fairies are more commonly called today, seem far more difficult to accept.

Only a couple of centuries ago fairies were seen as often as UFOs are reported nowadays. But before the Victorian era, fairies were not pictured as we view them today. It was only in the nineteenth century that they came to be seen as delicate winged entities. Previously, fairies were seen as very human-like, a little smaller than ourselves, but possessed of amazing powers. In Ireland one individual who encountered the fairy king on Halloween was reputed to have been blinded by a touch from a fairy wand. But fairies could do good as well as evil, and it was widely believed that people who kept on their good side would be 'looked after'.

Scotland's foremost expert on the fairy kingdom was the Reverend Robert Kirk. In the seventeenth century he wrote a book about his experiences, *The Secret Commonwealth,* which became a bestseller in its day. At the Fairy Knowe or Hill just outside Aberfoyle, the Reverend Kirk would regularly meet with his fairy friends, until one day he disappeared with them, never to return. You can visit the Fairy Knowe today—it is a haunting spot, where people still leave messages for the fairies on strips of cloth. If you have an illness the idea is to wrap the cloth around the affected part, make a wish to the fairies, and then hang the cloth from a tree on the summit of the knowe. As the cloth decays so the illness will fade away.

It is said that the name of Captain Kirk of *Star Trek* fame was inspired by Robert Kirk's experiences. Though unlikely, this does highlight the similarities between fairy entities and extraterrestrials—for one thing both types of entity are alleged to have abducted people. In the case of the fairies the abductees were typically taken below ground, where they would be amazed by the technology they were shown. Robert Kirk reported that the fairies had fires which burned continually, but without wood or coal. They had lights which shone from an object shaped like a lamp, but which needed no fuel. Astonishing to him, but not something that would surprise us, with our modern electrical appliances.

It is often assumed that aliens take their victims into spaceships and disappear into distant galaxies, but the truth is that most abductees have no idea where they are taken. They often find themselves inside strange rooms, but do not know where they have gone. Some have reported that they feel that they are inside a building rather than a UFO. Furthermore, many abductions start inside the home, and fairies were notorious for their ability to get into people's houses. There is a view that UFOs originate inside the Earth—that we are not dealing with inhabitants of other worlds, but with entities from our own Earth perhaps from another dimension. There is a long-held belief in the existence of a hidden world deep inside the Earth. It has various names: Agharti is one, a legendary land which Buddhists believe lies deep underground, but which is connected to every country by a system of caves and tunnels. Is this the land of the fairies?

Belief in fairies was seriously affected by the notorious events that took place in the village of Cottingly, near Bradford, in the early years of this century—events which virtually destroyed the credibility of the subject. In 1917 two cousins, sixteen-year-old Elsie Wright and ten-year-old Frances Griffiths, claimed that they had taken photographs of fairies they had met beside a local stream. These came to the attention of spiritualists—including the famous writer, and creator of Sherlock Holmes, Sir Arthur Conan Doyle. Doyle was a leading light in the Spiritualist Movement and a firm believer in the ability of photographers to capture the spirits of the dead on film. The pictures the girls had taken showed several fairies exactly as they were generally visualised by society at that time—hand-high winged figures, some of which were gnome-like in appearance. Even at the time the pictures were widely regarded as fakes. Conan Doyle himself was ridiculed in the press for accepting them as genuine, and belief in the existence of fairies sank to a low point from which it has never recovered.

Was the criticism justified? Partly. Unknown to Conan Doyle, the photographs were faked, crudely as it turned out, by a local photographer, but it was not until 1983 that Elsie publicly admitted the deception. The pictures themselves were a hoax, but Elsie went on to make a remarkable claim. She was adamant that she had seen real live fairies all those years before, and the hoax pictures had been created out of the sheer frustration of no-one believing her story. Little has changed in the intervening years, but although scorned as a subject for serious discussion, people continue to see nature spirits, particularly in Scotland.

One person who had many such contacts was the mystic, and founder of the Findhorn community, R. O. Crombie, whose experiences began one day in the summer of 1965. He was sitting in Edinburgh's Royal Botanic Garden when he suddenly became aware of a change in the atmosphere around him. Everything seemed to go still. Then he was astonished to see, standing a few yards away, a strange beast, half-human, half-horse. He immediately knew that what he was seeing was a mythical beast—a centaur. As the beast spoke to him Crombie became aware of other strange creatures, nature spirits, who gathered around him as news spread that here was a human who could see them. They told Crombie that they, the people known as fairies, could see us all the time, but only a few humans could see them. Why Robert Crombie suddenly gained this visual insight into another world is unclear.

Crombie's initial encounter may seem hard to take, but subsequent incidents defy belief. Strolling down The Mound in Edinburgh he claimed to have been accosted by an entity which he rapidly recognised as the nature god Pan. This strange being explained to Crombie that he was upset at being branded 'the Devil' by Christians.

In the Crombie tradition, Glasgow psychic Ian Shanes also has regular communication with these denizens of another world. On an expedition to Loch Morar, organised by the group Scottish Earth Mysteries Research, he visited one of the islands, Eilean Bàn. It is a haunting spot, lying a quarter of a mile off the western shore of the loch. Now thickly overgrown and uninhabited, it was home to a catholic seminary until 1713. Later, Jacobites fleeing from the defeat at Culloden hid on the island for several months, but it has been uninhabited ever since.

Yet it seems that what man gave up, the nature spirits have taken over. While on the island, Ian Shanes came across elf-type creatures, about the height of his wellington boots. Scrambling over a fallen tree, Ian spotted strange entities, a few inches in height, but with lizard-like tails and human heads.

The area around the loch seems to teem with these spirits of nature. At one spot Ian made contact with an elf child and learned that this particular area was under the control of elf folk. According to the account given by the elves, the small burns of this marshy landscape were used by them just as we use canals and rivers for transportation.

Evidence also emerged that the fairies do live underground, as, at one point, Shanes was drawn towards two small humps, from which a group of fairies appeared. They seemed shy at first, perhaps surprised that contact was being made with them. Gradually, however, they seemed to gain in confidence and moved towards Ian until they were at his feet. They were apparently bemused by the activities of their human visitor and, when Ian explained that he was hoping to see the mythical beast associated with Loch Morar, the fairies looked astonished and told him that all humans were indeed mad!

So are there really fairies at the bottom of our gardens? If there are other dimensions, who knows what creatures might be lurking there. If we are willing to take tales of loch monsters, aliens and ghosts seriously, is it any harder to believe in the existence of those little people we call fairies?

FILE NO: 026
SUBJECT: ....the Ringcroft poltergeist
LOCATION: ....Rerrick, Kirkcudbrightshire
DATE: ....February-April 1695
CLASSIFICATION: AN2/3
STATUS: .... open

'THE TROUBLE CAME OFTEN UPON THE HOUSE . . .'

One of the most remarkable manifestations of a poltergeist took place in Kirkcudbrightshire, at a farm called Ringcroft of Stocking in the parish of Rerrick. What was special about this event was the prolonged time over which the outbreak of activity occurred, and the fact that it was apparently seen and attested to by so many different witnesses. The events at Ringcroft of Stocking, which happened in 1695, were so extraordinary that they were written up and published the following year by the local minister, Alexander Telfer, and he, four other ministers, and a further nine adult men subscribed their names to the account, swearing the truth of the details. There were also many women and children, but in those days their testimony was not considered important.

For many years the case was cited in *Encyclopaedia Britannica* as a fine example of a poltergeist.

The farm was lived in by Andrew Mackie and his family. In February 1695, Mackie discovered one morning that some of his cattle had broken their tethers during the night. He retied them the following night with stronger bonds, but they broke loose again. Shortly after this someone or something piled up a stack of peats in the middle of the house, again at night, and set it alight. Luckily the family discovered the fire before any permanent damage was done.

At the beginning of March, a volley of stones was thrown at the house—but from where, no-one could tell. Showers of stones are quite common in poltergeist outbreaks of this kind. At Mackie's house, both inside and outside it, and in every room, stones would bombard the occupants from 7th March almost continually until the activity subsided at the end of April.

A few days later some of the children came in and saw what they thought was a strange figure sitting by the fire, covered in a blanket. It was not a person, however, but only a stool which had been turned upside down and the blanket placed over it. But again, who or what had positioned it like this was not discovered.

Kitchen implements, including pots and pans, went missing and would be found, after long hours of searching, in the most unlikely places—up in the loft, for example. The stone-throwing got worse. It seemed especially bad on Sundays. Whoever was leading family prayers on this day seemed to be targeted more than anybody else. It was after the first Sunday that Mackie took his troubles to the minister, Mr Telfer. Telfer visited a day or two later, and they discussed the possible causes of the activity. One explanation seemed more likely than any other.

Some years before, the house had been inhabited by a family called McNaught. The householder McNaught had a run of bad luck, including poor crop yields and ill health. He suspected his house might be cursed, and sent his son to visit a woman known for her ability to see into both the past and the future. The son went to the woman, but on his way home ran into a recruiting party, and either enlisted or was pressed into joining the army. He was sent to Flanders, where he met another young man from the same parish who was about to go home on leave. The son asked this man, John Redick, to pass on the woman's message to his father. There was a stone slab at the entrance to the house, which he must lift. Underneath it he would find a tooth. He must burn this. If he did not, his ill luck would continue.

Redick duly arrived with the message, only to find that McNaught's luck had run out completely and he was dead. Instead of telling the new tenant, a man called Thomas Telfer, Redick went to the minister, Alexander Telfer, and confided in him. The minister decided to do and say nothing, but Redick must have afterwards told other people, because word got around, and Thomas Telfer lifted the stone slab and found something below it, either a bit of tooth or bone, which he burnt. He never had any problems in the house, but when he moved out and Mackie moved in, problems certainly arose.

During his visit, the minister did not notice much untoward. A couple of stones struck him as he was leaving, but things seemed to have calmed down. Then, the following Sunday, a veritable shower of stones rained down. The minister arrived again the next week, to lead prayers, and was hit both by stones and by some invisible object like a great stick, that fairly loundered him about the shoulders. There were also loud rappings and knocks, and both the minister and other witnesses began to see apparitions of human figures, or parts of bodies, such as 'a little white hand and arm from the elbow down'.

Things got even worse in the days following. The landlord and some neighbours tried to enter the house and were beaten by sticks and struck by stones so fiercely that they had to retreat. Others were dragged around the house by their clothes, while bedclothes were pulled off the sleeping children, who were also mysteriously beaten on their hips, bits of furniture were lifted and moved, the beds and chests shook and trembled, and stones continued to rain down. A voice was heard saying, 'Wisht! Wisht!' which set the dog barking. When a group of local ministers arrived to drive out the Trouble, as it was now being called, they only seemed to aggravate matters. Rocks weighing up to eight pounds were launched at them. One minister was cut severely on the head and had his wig pulled off him. Fires were started spontaneously in the yard outside. The Mackies were in despair.

Then Mrs Mackie noticed a loose slab outside the door. She lifted it and found 'seven small bones, with blood, and some flesh, all closed in a piece of old suddled paper.' Very frightened, she ran for the landlord. While she was away the stone-throwing renewed with greater intensity, and fireballs landed in the house. The children's bedclothes were set alight, and the beds shaken again, accompanied by loud groaning. It was not until the bones found by Mrs Mackie were removed and sent to the minister that things subsided again.

The following is an extract from Alexander Telfer's account, which gives an indication of the terrifying events. This refers to 10th April, when, says the minister, the Trouble

> *came often with such force upon the house that it made all the house Shake, it brake an hole thorrow the Timber and Thatch of the House, and poured in great Stones, one whereof more then an Quarter weight fell upon Mr James Monteith his back, yet he was not hurt, it threw an other with great force at him when he was praying bigger than a Mans fist which hit him on the Breast yet he was neither hurt nor moved thereby . . . it Gripped, and Handled the Legs of some, as with a Mans hand; it Hoised up the feet of others while standing on the ground, thus it did to William Lennox of Mill-house, my Self and others, in this manner it continued till Ten a Clock at night.*

In mid-April the Mackies moved out, and some neighbours looked after the place. The disturbances died away. So the Mackies came home. The disturbances started up again. Now when someone was struck they could hear a voice saying, 'Take you that!' Fire-raising and stone-throwing continued, and mud was thrown at those in prayer. Finally a voice began to converse with Mackie. It seemed to be the voice of a spirit, and it said he would be troubled for a further four days. When Mackie asked who had sent the spirit, it replied that God had sent it, to warn the land to repent: 'for a judgment is to come if the land do not quickly repent, and I will return a hundred time worse upon every family in the land.' But then the voice also said that if Mackie prayed to it and worshipped it, it would trouble him no more.

Mackie, recognising the tempting voice of the Devil, refused. The next day the house was fired seven times, and family and neighbours slaved all day to extinguish the flames. Finally, on 30th April, the landlord led prayers in the byre. The spirit had been promising that their troubles would soon be over, and as the gathered people prayed, they saw 'a black thing' in one corner, which slowly grew like a cloud until it filled the whole room, and from which chaff and mud was flung at them. It seemed to be able to grip some of them around their waists and arms, making them cry out in pain, and leaving marks on them that would last for days. But then the cloud dispersed and all was quiet.

The next day a small building used to keep sheep in was set on fire and burnt to the ground, but this seemed to be the last act of the Trouble. Thereafter the Mackies lived on in peace. The whole incident, as it was described in Telfer's *A True Relation of an Apparition, Expressions and Actings of a*

Spirit, which infested the house of Andrew Mackie in Ringcroft of Stocking, in the paroch of Rerrick, in the Stewartry of Kirkcudbrightshire, remains one of the most bizarre recorded events in the annals of Scottish history.

SECTION III

DARK SECRETS

FILE NO: 027
SUBJECT: ....Boleskine House/Aleister Crowley
LOCATION: ....nr. Foyers, Loch Ness
DATE: .... 1900 onwards
CLASSIFICATION: AN3
STATUS: .... open

THE WICKEDEST MAN IN THE WORLD

It was the search for an oratory—a private, secluded place for meditation, prayer and esoteric ritual—which, as the 20th century dawned, led a young man northwards, to a large house surrounded by two acres of land in the Highlands of Scotland.

Boleskine House, built in the 18th century by Archibald Fraser, a relative of Lord Lovat, lies on a wooded hillside on the eastern side of Loch Ness, close by the village of Foyers. The new occupant was Aleister Crowley, who had already, at the age of 25, begun to carve a name for himself as a master of the occult.

Both his parents were devout members of the Plymouth Brethren, and from an early age Crowley had been taught of the terrible power of unearthly forces. Passages from the Bible, in particular images from the Book of Revelation, haunted him, so that in later life he would call himself 'The Beast', a name which he claimed had been cast upon him by his mother, and the notion of the 'Scarlet Woman'—the whore of Babylon—was to colour his many relationships throughout his life. Indeed, he went out of his way to defy all conventions of morality—hence his description of himself as 'the wickedest man in the world'.

Crowley had rebelled against his strict Christian background while an undergraduate at Cambridge, where he read moral science. Though he left the university without gaining his degree, he did manage to have two books of poetry published—one satanic, and the other pornographic, the latter work having to be printed abroad.

A keen and courageous mountaineer—he was said to thrive on the thrill of danger—Crowley was in Switzerland during the summer after leaving Cambridge when he encountered an English chemist, J. L. Baker, with whom he attempted to discuss alchemy. Baker knew little about the ancient mysteries of the alchemists, but was able to put Crowley in touch with a friend who was a member of a covert magical sect called the Hermetic Order of the Golden Dawn. It was a turning point in Crowley's life, and he was not slow to immerse himself in the secrets of the Golden Dawn [*see also File No. 035*].

Within two years Crowley had become a leading member of the sect, and wanted solitude in order to further his training. He had scoured the Lake District, but settled upon Boleskine House as the most suitable site for his dark purposes. A north-facing room was called for, with a door opening on to a terrace strewn with sand—he was able to obtain all the sand he needed from the loch-side—and at the end of the terrace a lodge, within which evil spirits could gather.

And gather, it seemed, they did. Crowley wrote of his experiments in raising spirits, declaring that his success was so great that things got out of hand, and destructive forces were unleashed whose influence spread into both the house and the surrounding countryside. He claimed that one of the workmen on his land became deranged and attempted to kill him; that his coachman, a non-drinker, began to suffer from *delirium tremens*; and that his housekeeper disappeared, too terrified to remain in the house. The wider influence was revealed when Crowley carelessly wrote down the names of two demons on a bill from the local butcher. Soon after, while cutting meat for a customer, the butcher severed an artery and bled to death.

But this was only the beginning of Crowley's activities at Boleskine House. He reputedly held black masses there, indulged in orgies and obscene rituals, and many are the tales of weird happenings involving sex, magic rituals, alcohol, drugs and madness. 'Chaos magic'—the opening of one's mind to all influences, regardless of the consequences, in an effort to confront, control and manipulate the powers of darkness—was practised *in extremis* by Crowley.

Some of his less unusual activities also provoked a response from local people. Shortly after his arrival, Crowley recalled in his autobiographical *Confessions*, 'I innocently frightened some excellent people by my habit of taking long walks over the moors. One morning I found a large stone jar at my front door. It was not an infernal machine; it was illicit whisky—a mute, yet eloquent appeal not to give away illicit stills that I might happen to stumble across in my rambles. I needed no bribe. I am a free trader in every sense of the word.'

The house itself, which was later owned by Jimmy Page, guitarist with Led Zeppelin, is reputed to be haunted, although this may be due as much to Crowley's reputation as anything. A poltergeist, which removes and later replaces items, is one of its supposed spirits. According to legend, an underground tunnel connects the house with Boleskine burial ground, across the road on the shores of the loch, which contains the ruins of the old kirk and many ancient gravestones. Witches are said to haunt the burial ground.

However, the subsequent owners of Boleskine House, Ronald and Annette MacGillivary, dismissed any notion that the house is haunted. In an article in the *Daily Record*, Mrs MacGillivary described the stories as 'a load of bunkum'. They had never had a disturbed night in the five years since they had bought it. She explained that the house's reputation was more of an irritation than anything else, as Crowley's admirers still regard it as a kind of mecca.

Jimmy Page, who owned Boleskine for twenty years from the 1970s, never lived there himself, but rented it to a friend,

Malcolm Dent. Dent retains a healthy respect for the house's ill-repute, claiming that he had had a few scary moments there himself, and that nothing about the place would surprise him.

McX
028

FILE NO: 028
SUBJECT: .... air crash/Duke of Kent
LOCATION: ....nr. Berriedale, Caithness
DATE: .... August 1942
CLASSIFICATION: .... n/a
STATUS: ....classified

TRAGEDY AT EAGLE'S ROCK

The mist was thick on the coast of Caithness on Tuesday 25th August 1942. The cloud was dense and low over most of northern Scotland that day, from the Moray Firth to the Pentland Firth. It was, in fact, only once the mainland of Scotland was left behind that bright sunshine dominated again, over the flat calm sea as far as Orkney and beyond. Was the unusually poor visibility responsible for one of the strangest and most dramatic flying accidents of the Second World War? Or was some other factor involved?

These are the facts, as far as they are known: some time between one and two in the afternoon of the 25th, a shepherd and his son, David and Hugh Morrison, heard the sound of an aeroplane flying low over their heads on the high ground inland from the village of Berriedale. Seconds later there was an enormous explosion. The men could see nothing, but it was clear that they were the nearest human beings to the site of a terrible crash. They raised the alarm, as did a fisherman further up the Berriedale Water, and soon search parties from Dunbeath, Berriedale and further afield were out on the moors, looking for the wreckage and any survivors.

The mist severely hampered the search, but there was an intense smell of burning aviation fuel which led a local farmer, James Sutherland, to be the first on the scene. The wreckage was of an RAF Sunderland flying-boat, and it was spread over the slopes of a high bluff known as Eagle's Rock. There were several bodies lying in the vicinity, and others trapped in the plane itself. But there were, it appeared, no survivors.

A local doctor, a man of seventy called Dr Kennedy, arrived at the isolated spot after crossing several miles of boggy moorland. There were 14 bodies in all, which Kennedy examined in turn. One of these wore the uniform of an Air Commodore. His face was familiar to several of the rescuers, and his identity bracelet confirmed what they feared: the bracelet bore the words, 'His Royal Highness The Duke of Kent, The Coppins, Iver, Buckinghamshire'. The Duke was the younger brother of King George VI. His body was draped in an opened parachute, and later it was taken to the Duke of Sutherland's castle at Dunrobin, whence it was transferred by train to London.

The Sunderland, number W-4026, had taken off from the naval base near Invergordon, in the Cromarty Firth, at 1.10 p.m. It was due to fly to Iceland, where the Duke of

Kent, whose responsibilities were for the welfare of RAF personnel in various locations, was to visit some of the airmen who formed part of the occupying forces there. It was a long flight, and the flying-boat carried 2,500 gallons of fuel. This had ignited when the plane hit the hillside.

The searchers were all exhausted and in varying states of shock at what they saw. One of them, a policeman from Wick called Carter, maintained that he had heard a human voice calling in distress from somewhere not far away. Everybody stopped to listen, and again made a search of the surrounding area. But nobody was found. Indeed, it was hard to believe that anybody could have survived, let alone walked away from, the devastation before them.

However, the RAF revealed that there should have been 15 men on board the flight. The day after the crash, a woman in a cottage at Rinsarry, several miles from the site of the crash, was amazed to see a barefoot, dazed, bloody and burnt man stagger into her garden and collapse. This was Flight-Sergeant Andrew Jack, the 21-year-old rear gunner of the plane. 'I am an airman and our plane has crashed. I am the only survivor,' he said.

The tail-turret of the Sunderland, it could be seen from the wreckage, had broken off on impact and Jack had been thrown clear. He had attempted to look for his comrades, pulled some of the bodies out of the burning plane, and then set off for help. Not surprisingly, in the mist and on the unfamiliar rough hillside, injured and in a state of shock, he had lost his way entirely. More surprising was the fact that he had survived the night at all. He was despatched to the hospital at Lybster, where he was visited by officials from the RAF trying to piece together what had happened. All that Andrew Jack was able to recall were the words of his captain and pilot Flight Lieutenant Frank Goyen before the crash: 'Let's go down and have a look.' He seemed to think that these words had been uttered about ten minutes after take-off.

The Sunderland was a notoriously cumbersome and heavy plane. It took off in a dead calm sea in the Cromarty Firth and, according to Jack, had to make an abnormally long run before hitting a wave big enough to get it off the water. Standard procedure with flying-boats was to make as much of any flight as possible take place over water. As the rate of climb, especially with a full load on board, could be as little as 200 feet per minute, the usual route from Cromarty to Iceland would have been to head north-east out through the Moray Firth, gaining height slowly over the sea, and then to turn north-west once the tip of Caithness was reached. This would avoid the hazards of the 3,000-foot mountains of the north-west, and more particularly the steep rising land just inland from the east coast.

In fact, we do not know whether the plane deviated from this or any other recognised flight path because the flight plan for this particular journey has never been disclosed by the RAF. It has simply disappeared. However, Frank Goyen, the captain and pilot, was the man shouldered with the blame for the crash by the official report, which was made to the House of Commons by Sir Archibald Sinclair on 7th October, and specifically he was blamed because 'the aircraft was flown on a track other than that indicated in the flight plan given to the pilot, and at too low an altitude to clear the rising ground of the track.' The responsibility for this 'serious mistake' lay with the captain. But the report also contained a sentence which seemed to undermine its own argument: 'the weather encountered should have presented no difficulties to an experienced pilot'. And it went on, 'the examination of the propellers showed that the engines were under power when the aircraft struck the ground, and . . . all the occupants of the aircraft were on duty at the time of the accident.'

This was the difficulty. Apart from the thick mist, there was nothing untoward about the weather conditions. No experienced pilot, as the report itself admitted, should have had a problem. And Goyen was extremely experienced. He was an Australian, 25 years old, highly regarded by his crew and others and with almost 1,000 operational hours to his credit. He was accompanied by Wing Commander T. L. Mosley, Commanding Officer of 228 Squadron (to which the Sunderland was attached), another highly experienced pilot, and there were a further two pilots on board, Pilot Officer S. W. Smith, acting second officer, and Pilot Officer G. R. Saunders, the navigator. Even Andrew Jack, who had flown many times with Goyen, had made the Iceland trip more than once before. It was a team befitting its important passenger, for 'Georgie', the Prince, the flamboyant husband of the beautiful Princess Marina, was himself an enthusiastic and experienced pilot.

What, then, went wrong? The most frequently given explanation is that Goyen and his crew opted to head out along the Moray Firth, stay over water, and not turn until they reached the clearer skies over the Pentland Firth. Somehow, Goyen, his co-pilots and his navigator were all unaware that they were drifting westward, and had crossed the coast around Berriedale and were heading straight towards the high ground, which the Sunderland was not able to clear. This seems extraordinary. In such conditions, in any case, the rule would have been to maintain and indeed gain height. What of the pilot's remark, as heard by Andrew Jack, 'Let's go down and have a look'? Surely this could not be interpreted as meaning, 'The mist is so thick we can't see where we are, let's go down and have a look.' This would run counter to all safety procedures. In any case, the crew knew that the mist was right down nearly to sea-level. So could there have been something else they were looking for or at? If so, what? The aircraft was loaded with depth-charges in case enemy submarines were spotted, but surely, only ten minutes into the flight, this could not have been what was meant.

Andrew Jack, the only survivor, might have provided some answers, but he never did. While recovering in hospital he was visited by senior officers from the RAF and it is generally thought that he was officially 'silenced' by being made to sign the Official Secrets Act. It was not until years later that he began making statements disputing the official inquiry's line that pilot error was to blame. He died in 1978, still convinced that responsibility could not be laid at the door of Frank Goyen. Perhaps he felt an added loyalty to Goyen who, on the morning of the flight, had for some reason given him a signed photograph of himself with the message 'With memories of happier days'. Was there some significance to this unexpected message? Did Goyen know or suspect something about the flight that he could not divulge in any other way?

In 1985 the writer Robin McWhirter prepared a radio documentary on the whole affair, *The Crash of W-4026*, and in the course of his researches he came up with a number of unanswered questions. Among these were: why did 228 Squadron's record book give the time of the crash as 2 p.m., when the plane took off at 1.10 p.m. and had been flying for a maximum of 30 minutes when it crashed? The plane's own clock had stopped at 1.30 p.m., presumably on impact, and although it has never been confirmed, the Duke of Kent's watch had also stopped, it is said, a few minutes after that time. Also, was it simply clerical error at the House of Commons that Hansard recorded the accident as having occurred on 15th August, not the 25th? Why is all the official documentation surrounding the inquiry missing? Why do the Public Record Office, the RAF and the Royal Archives at Windsor all deny having any records relating to the crash? After all, the Duke was fifth in line to the throne. The keeper of records at Windsor apparently said that he was 'not permitted to release the very few other documents which are of relevance.'

Could there in short be some other, more sinister, reason behind the crash? The death of the Duke was a blow to morale—could it have been the work of an enemy saboteur? Or, indeed, of a home-grown saboteur? There were rumours that the Duke of Kent, like the Duke of Windsor and other members of the royal family, was 'sympathetic to an understanding with Germany'. Might it have been felt necessary to have him removed? The war was at a crucial stage, with the tide beginning to turn in the Allies' favour. The last thing Churchill's government would have wanted was a slackening of the resolve to defeat Germany totally.

This seems like an extreme example of conspiracy theory, but in the absence of satisfactory official explanations such speculation is inevitable. Other theories have included technical explanations such as the effect of magnetic rocks on the plane's compass, or of down-draught which forced it too low. Again, as the defence writer Malcolm Spaven, in a letter to *The Scotsman* pointed out, the loss of Sunderlands by accident was far from rare during the war: some 80 were lost, only two of them shot down by the enemy, and there were 15 crashes similar to that involving the Duke in the same general area. Of these, 12 caused fatalities, a total of 77. These statistics do seem to make it much more likely that, in spite of the wealth of experience of the crew, either pilot error or mechanical failure might well have been the cause of the loss of W-4026.

This letter was written in response to an article by Robin McWhirter that appeared in *The Scotsman* at the end of August 1985 as a preview to his radio programme. A number of other letters appeared as a result, among which the most interesting came from Richard Fresson. He was the son of the late Captain E. E. Fresson, who had been ordered by the RAF, the day after the crash, to check out the location of the wreckage from the air, and he quoted his father's recollections of the 25th, the day of the crash. On that day Captain Fresson had been on a flight from Inverness to Kirkwall. The Meteorological Office reported poor conditions all the way as far as the Pentland Firth, where they improved. (This information, of course, would also have been available to Frank Goyen and his crew.)

'We flew north,' wrote Fresson, 'above the cloud at 4,000 feet and found the Pentland Firth bathed in sunshine with the sea looking a deep emerald green. We departed from Kirkwall around one o'clock in the afternoon on the return trip and flew around the west side of Hoy across to Thurso in sunny weather. We caught up with the low cloud again at Thurso, where I turned off on the south-easterly course to bring the plane over Dunbeath on the Caithness coastline and which we passed over above cloud at 1.30 p.m.

'At approximately the same time as we departed from Kirkwall, the Sunderland flying-boat took off from the Cromarty Firth. . . .

'For some unknown reason, after being airborne for barely ten minutes, the captain was heard by the rear gunner over the intercom to say. "Let's go down and have a look". Knowing as he must have done that there was a very low ceiling on the first part of the trip, I never understood what possessed the captain to take such unnecessary risks. He only had to fly on course for another ten minutes and he would have had the whole of the Pentland Firth in view.

'However, down they went and at about 200 feet they broke cloud to find themselves in a narrow valley, running parallel to the coastline, north of the village of Berriedale. That valley extends roughly three miles northwards and at the end the ground rises sharply up from near sea level to a thousand feet. With the poor visibility, the pilot evidently failed to see the sharply-rising ground in time. The aircraft clock found in the wreckage had stopped at half-past one, the time I was actually flying overhead and changing course for Inverness.'

Even Captain Fresson, flying in almost the same location (but at a safe height) at precisely the same time, could not offer a satisfactory explanation for the pilot's actions. Neither could anybody else, before or since. Robin McWhirter, in a subsequent letter to *The Scotsman*, concluded: 'There is much more I could write about the crew of W-4026, but I will limit myself to one sentence: Whatever caused the tragedy at Eagle's Rock, it wasn't pilot error.'

FILE NO: 029
SUBJECT: .... Rosslyn Chapel/Knights Templar
LOCATION: ....Roslin, Midlothian
DATE: .... c. 1086 to present
CLASSIFICATION: .... n/a
STATUS: .... pending

THE KNIGHTS, THE CROSS AND THE SHROUD

Rosslyn Chapel is a unique building, its origins and significance wreathed in mystery and ancient tradition—both Christian and pagan. Situated close to the village of Roslin in Midlothian, the building of the chapel was begun in 1447 by William St Clair, Prince of Orkney, and ever since then strange rumours and legends have grown up about the place.

The St Clairs were a long-established and powerful family, occupying a massive castle that towered over the valley of the River Esk. They had been closely associated with the Scottish crown since the battle of Bannockburn in 1314. Strangely, at around the same time as work on the chapel was begun, evil omens were noted, apparently prophesying disaster for the family. Almost immediately, the fortunes of the St Clairs went into decline—a serious fire destroying much of their once-splendid castle. But this was to be only the first in a series of misfortunes which befell the St Clairs over the next three hundred years.

For such a relatively small building, the chapel has been the subject of an enormous amount of speculation over the years. It has even been suggested that it was intended to be an exact replica of the ruined Temple of Solomon—an ancient site of great mystical significance, and the original base of the Knights Templar in 12th-century Jerusalem.

Acclaimed as one of the finest examples of Gothic architecture in Britain, the exterior of the chapel remains unfinished, and it is the extravagantly ornate interior that has secured its reputation as one of the finest examples of the medieval mason's art. It is filled with a mass of exquisite carving and decoration of every description, depicting biblical themes—such as The Seven Deadly Sins and The Dance of Death—alongside imagery often associated with the 'Green Man', the ancient pagan symbolic figure. Its most interesting feature, however, is the so-called 'Apprentice Pillar'.

The darker side of the chapel's story begins with this extraordinary piece of craftsmanship, and a tale of jealousy and murder. The pillar's creator, a young apprentice who carved it while the master mason was away, is said to have been murdered in the chapel by his master in a fit of jealousy shortly after it was completed. At the south-west corner, high up on the wall, a carved head with a wound on its forehead is reputed to depict the murdered apprentice.

In recent times it has been the vault beneath the chapel, rather than the chapel itself, that has been the subject of the greatest speculation. It is possible that this vault was modelled on the one beneath the Temple of Solomon, reputed to have been excavated by the Templars in the 12th century and only rediscovered by British army engineers in the 1860s. At various times it has been claimed that The Holy Grail, The True Cross of Christ, or Holy Rood as it was known, the Ark of the Covenant and even—most bizarre of all—the remains of a UFO, lie buried in the vault at Rosslyn. The substance of these rumours is difficult to establish, as the vault has been sealed for more than three centuries, and the current guardians of the chapel, the 7th Earl of Rosslyn and his family, are said to have no plans to investigate these claims.

The link with the True Cross or Holy Rood, at least, seems to be partly based on historical events. The St Clair family may well have an association with the Holy Rood dating back almost a thousand years. A piece of the Holy Rood was brought back to Scotland from Hungary by Queen Margaret in 1086, and the man entrusted with its safekeeping was called St Clair. From this date on, the story of the Holy Rood is confused—apparently seized by Edward I in 1296, it was later returned to Scotland, only to be removed by the English again in the 14th century and taken to Durham Cathedral. Yet by the middle of the 15th century the Rood was back in Scotland once more, in the hands of the St Clair family and safely housed in the vault at Rosslyn Chapel. Shadowy links with the Knights Templar—the monastic military order founded during the Crusades—suggest that they may well have played a part in the movements of the Rood.

Most recently, the story of the chapel's links with the Templars and the secrets of the vault have taken another extraordinary turn. Christopher Knight and Robert Lomas, in their book *The Second Messiah,* claim that the vault is the resting place of a number of ancient scrolls, discovered beneath the ruins of the Temple of Solomon in Jerusalem by the original Knights Templar between 1118 and 1128. After the suppression of the Templars in the 14th century, these scrolls are said to have been brought to Rosslyn and interred in the vault. Although backed up by a number of interesting discoveries—including a strange carving apparently depicting a Templar initiating a candidate into the first degree of Freemasonry—the assertion that the vault contains the ancient scrolls cannot be proved. Until the vault is opened. And it does not seem likely this will happen in the near future.

One other intriguing connection Knight and Lomas make is that between the chapel and the Turin Shroud. A carving inside the chapel seems to depict a headless figure holding up a cloth on which a face, remarkably similar to that on the Turin Shroud, can be seen. They also suggest that the image on the shroud is not that of Christ, but that of Jaques de Molay, last Grand Master of the Templars, who was executed for heresy in 1307.

Whatever the truth of this assertion, it does seem clear that there is a connection between Rosslyn Chapel, The Knights

Templar, and the Freemasons—classic elements in all the most bizarre conspiracy theories of recent times.

Perhaps we will never know the exact significance of this extraordinary building, or the extent of its founder's involvement with the secret history of the Templars. And until the vault is opened, the truth or otherwise of the claims made about its hidden treasures will remain an intriguing mystery.

FILE NO: 030
SUBJECT: ....the monster of Glamis
LOCATION: .... Glamis Castle
DATE: ....c. 1821 to 1920
CLASSIFICATION: AN3
STATUS: .... open

A TERRIBLE SECRET

The ancient castle of Glamis, near Forfar in Angus, is the seat of the Earls of Strathmore and Kinghorne, and the childhood home of Elizabeth Bowes-Lyon, the Queen Mother. Its long and bloody history has given it many legendary and ghostly associations. It has been said that of all the great castles of Scotland, none boasts so many hauntings as Glamis. The building itself has been much altered over the centuries, not least in the 1770s, when the outer defences of walls and gateways were removed and rebuilt at a distance from the castle, to create a landscaped effect in the style of Capability Brown. This was done, as Sir Walter Scott angrily remarked, 'to render this splendid old mansion more parkish, as he pleased to call it.' But in spite of the changes, much of the medieval fortress remains to this day: some of the walls are up to fifteen feet thick. In such a place, mysterious tales persist—tales of one Earl 'Beardie' and his games of cards with the Devil, of a room of skulls where a band of Ogilvies were locked away and left to starve to death, of a terrifying giant with a long flowing beard, of a ghostly page-boy who trips up visitors as they pass by him, and of a grey lady in the 17th-century chapel. But no mystery has gripped the public imagination, and resulted in so much speculation, as that of the so-called Monster of Glamis.

The basis of this legend is that the family—or at least successive heads of it—have long lived with a terrible secret. At some time in the 19th century, it is said, a malformed child was born at Glamis. Some accounts say it was shaped 'like an egg', with tiny misshapen limbs and virtually no neck. It was expected—and no doubt hoped—that such a creature would not survive infancy, but on the contrary it grew big and strong. What was to be done with it? The answer was that it would live out its life far from the public gaze, in the seclusion of the deepest recesses of the castle. Meanwhile, as far as guests and visitors were concerned, life would proceed as normal.

Records show that in December 1820, Thomas, Lord Glamis, the son and heir of the 11th Earl, married one Charlotte Grimstead. On 22nd September 1822, as recorded in Burke's *Peerage*, she gave birth to a son, called Thomas George. Thomas George would in due course become the 12th Earl. There was, then, a gap of 22 months between the marriage and the birth. Both Douglas's *Scots Peerage* and

Cockayne's *Complete Peerage*, on the other hand, reveal a curiosity: in October of 1821, 11 months before Thomas George's birth, another son had been born, who died within a day or two (the dates in the two books differ slightly).

The suggestion made by some researchers is that this child, horribly malformed, did not in fact die, and that the records only reflect the family's fervent hope and intention, that, since they could not countenance such an unfortunate creature becoming heir to the earldom, it would be cared for until such time as it passed away. But it did not pass away. It grew to an immense size, barrel-shaped and hairy, but with almost useless arms and legs. It lived to a great age, and was kept, locked away for most of its life, in a private part of the huge castle.

This time it is the castle's *Book of Records* that offers a clue as to where such a place might have been. In 1684 the third Earl of Strathmore, Patrick, had a 'closet' built 'within the charter-house' by 'digging down from the floor of the littil pantry off the lobbis'—a closet which, with considerable difficulty in the construction, could also be accessed 'off one floor from the East quarter of the house . . . to the West side . . . thorrow the long hall'. This may or may not have been where the monster, if he existed, spent his life.

There are other possibilities, especially in the upper storeys. If he was well looked after, as seems to have been the case (apart from being deprived of his liberty), he would have required some exercise. There is a section of the roof still known as 'The Mad Earl's Walk'. Here, perhaps, he was taken at night and allowed a small measure of freedom.

Who knew of this secret? The mother, Charlotte Grimstead, presumably, unless she was somehow persuaded that her first child really had died while she was still recovering from the birth. Thomas, Lord Glamis, certainly, and of course his father, the Earl. With the birth of Thomas George, and then in 1824 of another son, Claude, the family could at least rest easy that the line of succession was secure. But equally clearly, as each heir reached his majority, they would need to be informed of the secret the castle contained. Somebody would also have to be entrusted with looking after the monster. A servant? Or was this done by the men of the family themselves. The only other people who seem to have been let in on what was going on were, for obvious reasons, the family lawyer and the factor. For two centuries, from the 1760s to the 1940s, only two families served as factors to the estate. It is easier to keep a secret when it becomes ritualised, passed in trust from father to son.

The colour brochure that visitors to Glamis can buy contains a family tree and a brief history of the various Earls and what they did. The tree is strangely barren in the way it represents Thomas, Lord Glamis (the supposed father of the monster). In the accompanying history, he is passed over completely. He died before his father, so his son Thomas George inherited the earldom, but he died in 1865 without issue. He too does not rate a mention in the history. One wonders why the coyness about this period. The 13th Earl was his brother Claude, who lived till 1904, and he was in turn succeeded by his son Claude (1855-1944) as 14th Earl.

Visitors to the castle in the 19th century frequently told stories of mysterious bangs and thumps in the dead of night, and one or two of catching glimpses of the enormous bearded giant. In recent generations the tradition of handing down the secret, if there was one, has died out: neither the present Earl nor his father were privy to it. When the Queen Mother's mother asked the factor of her day, Mr Gavin Ralston, to tell her the whole story, he only shook his head and replied, 'Lady Strathmore, it is fortunate you do not know it and will never know it, for if you did you would never be happy.'

Previous Earls have seldom been happy men, according to reports of their house-guests. Thomas George, the 12th Earl, was quoted as saying: 'If you could only guess the nature of the secret, you would go down on your knees and thank God it was not yours!' Augustus Hare, a man who spent much of his life enjoying the hospitality of country houses throughout Great Britain, describing a house-party at Glamis in 1877, wrote that Claude, the 13th Earl, had 'an ever-sad look'. The Queen Mother's sister, Lady Granville, once told James Wentworth Day that as a child she was forbidden to discuss the matter or ask anything about it. Lord Halifax, the author of a famous book on ghosts, was told by a family friend that when the 12th Earl died and the factor initiated his brother into the secret, Claude went to his wife and said, 'My dearest, you know how often we have joked over the secret room and the family mystery. I have been into the room; I have heard the secret; and if you wish to please me you will *never* mention the subject to me again.'

Lord Halifax also records that a number of alterations were made to the castle around this time. A workman accidentally came upon a door leading into a long passage. He became 'alarmed' at what he found down the passage and informed the Clerk of Works, who in turn notified the Lord Strathmore, who was then in London, and his lawyer in Edinburgh, by wire. All work was stopped immediately. The Earl and lawyer arrived and interrogated the workman. He was subsequently persuaded, and indeed paid, to emigrate.

There is also the story of the party of guests who, one day when the Earl was absent, decided to try to locate the 'secret room'. They went through the house, entering every room and hanging a towel out of every possible window. Then they went outside to see if there was a window without a towel. Apparently, high up in the walls, there was one small shuttered window that had no banner fluttering from it. But at this point the Earl and his lady unexpectedly returned, and coldly decreed that the experiment was over. And so the mystery was deepened, but not solved. And although the monster must now be long dead (some reports suggest that he lived until around 1920, having survived all those who planned his reclusive life for him) because the family resolutely and absolutely refuse to discuss the matter to this day, it persists in the public memory.

FILE NO: 031
SUBJECT: ....death of Willie McRae
LOCATION: ....nr. Loch Loyne
DATE: .... April 1985
CLASSIFICATION: .... n/a
STATUS: .... open

'NO SUSPICIOUS CIRCUMSTANCES'

It was ten in the morning of Saturday, 6th April 1985, on the A87 road, which runs from Invergarry past Loch Garry and Loch Loyne to Kyle of Lochalsh. At the height of summer this Highland route is usually busy with holiday traffic. It was the Easter weekend, and so there were already a few cars going in both directions. An Australian tourist and his wife suddenly spotted something red, about seventy yards off the road down the steep slope that ends in Loch Loyne. The couple assumed it was an abandoned vehicle. It was only when they had driven on a mile or two that they began to have doubts, and turned back. Their worst fears were confirmed when they saw a maroon Volvo, lying in a burn, its rear window shattered, the driver's window wound down but the door wedged shut against the bank of the burn.

Inside, the driver sat slumped in his seat, blood oozing from his head.

The Australian tourist rushed back up to the road and waved down the first vehicle that came along. There were four occupants—David Coutts, a Dundee councillor and member of the Scottish National Party, his wife Alison, and their friends Dr Dorothy Messer and George Lochhead. They hurried down to see what they could do. Another vehicle drove on to find a telephone and get emergency help.

David Coutts was astonished, on reaching the Volvo, to recognise the man who lay inside it. It was another member of the SNP, Willie McRae, a maverick figure well-known for his bullish and sometimes idiosyncratic behaviour. It appeared that his car had left the road, perhaps taking the bend too fast, and ended up where it was after careering down the slope. Dr Messer took the victim's pulse. McRae was still alive, although in a state of coma. The car-keys were lying in his lap.

An ambulance and the police arrived. McRae was removed from the car and taken to hospital in Inverness. Later he was transferred to Aberdeen Royal Infirmary, where he died the following day. But what was surprising was the discovery, not publicly revealed for two days, that he had not died of injuries sustained in a car crash. What killed Willie McRae was a .22 bullet wound to the head.

Willie McRae was a veteran campaigner for the SNP. Born in 1923 near Falkirk, he joined the party while still at school, became a vice-chairman and stood three times (unsuccessfully) as a Parliamentary candidate for Ross and Cromarty, a constituency he nearly won from the Conservatives in 1974. Before that he had studied history at Glasgow University, joined the Seaforth Highlanders, and then transferred to the Royal Indian Navy. He was the youngest captain in the RIN, learned Urdu and Hindi, and extended his nationalist views to become fervently in favour of Indian independence. At the end of the Second World War he moved to Naval Intelligence. There is speculation that he may have used his knowledge and position to further the cause of Indian independence, maintaining secret contact with the Indian National Congress, and thus learned early on some of the tricks of the trade of British undercover operations. However, it has also been pointed out that between 1945 and 1946, when this allegedly occurred, there was no doubt in anybody's mind that Indian independence was going to happen: it was simply a question of how, and when.

In any event, before 1946 was out, McRae had left India and was back in Glasgow studying for a second degree in law. He had a successful legal career, but also managed to continue his political activism. He was certainly in sympathy, if not actually involved, with those students who took the Stone of Destiny from Westminster Abbey in 1950. He helped the new state of Israel to frame some of its maritime laws and kept up his contacts in India and Pakistan as well as other parts of the world, often places where peoples and nations were emerging from the shadow of colonial rule.

Although based in Glasgow, McRae had a love of the Highlands, and bought himself a holiday cottage near Dornie, in Wester Ross. His characteristically blunt manner, his refusal to be cowed by the arguments of people with whom he disagreed, made him both admired and feared in political circles. He was seen by some as indiscreet, erratic and stubborn: even those who knew him well were sometimes surprised by his choice of causes and the enthusiasm which he showed for them. But even those who disliked him were in no doubt of his passion, commitment and genuinely held beliefs. In 1980, when there had been much opposition (from the SNP and others) to proposed test-drilling for sites for the storage of nuclear waste in the Mullwharchar Hills of Ayrshire, McRae was foremost in the campaign to stop the drilling. He represented the SNP at a four-week public inquiry held at Ayr, which resulted in the plans being abandoned. McRae memorably suggested that if nuclear waste was to be stored anywhere, it should go where Guy Fawkes had put his gunpowder.

The Atomic Energy Authority's plans had been thwarted in Ayrshire, but in the early '80s it became apparent to interested groups that it had not given up its search for suitable sites for waste disposal. One of these was rumoured to be in Glen Etive, near Oban. A caravan was set up in the glen, manned by members of the militant nationalist group Siol nan Gaidheal (Seed of the Gael) the idea being to maintain a constant presence in case any secret test-drilling went ahead. Geologists entering Glen Etive on AEA business were threatened and so were landowners who allowed them on to their land. McRae had links with some of the people involved in Siol nan Gaidheal, an organisation frowned upon by the many in the SNP, especially those on the left, who disliked what they saw as its militaristic and right-wing characteristics. Eventually the SNP would make membership of SnG incompatible with party membership. Willie McRae, perhaps seeing the writing on the wall, dissociated himself from the group. He could not, he explained to a friend, condone the violent tendencies of some members.

McRae's name has been linked since his death with other extreme nationalist forces, such as the Scottish National Liberation Army, which ran a letter-bomb campaign against Conservative politicians in the period 1982-85. There is no evidence that McRae had any direct involvement with the SNLA, but he may have known some of the individuals involved. He may also have known who was involved in the Dark Harvest Commando of the Scottish Citizen Army, a shadowy group which in 1981 removed soil from the anthrax-infested island of Gruinard, Wester Ross, and sent some of it back to Porton Down Laboratories in Wiltshire, where the original anthrax spores had been cultivated during germ warfare experiments in the Second World War. But again, there is no hard evidence for this, other than the fact that McRae was familiar with the more extreme tendencies of the nationalist movement in Scotland.

Given the tiny number of individuals involved in such activities, however—usually written off as sad and lonely 'nutters' by mainstream nationalists—it seems unlikely that a man as deeply involved in the SNP as McRae was would have had more than a passing interest in such people. It is also true, though, that in the reactionary mood of the 1980s, British intelligence on all Scottish political activity, especially on the fringes, became quite intense. McRae was almost certainly 'watched' and at one time apparently knew by sight some of those observing him, as they turned up regularly to meetings he was attending or addressing.

When, after his admission to hospital, the cause of McRae's head-wound was established, the police naturally returned to the scene of the 'accident' and had a fresh look. This was the following day, by which time helpers, onlookers, ambulancemen, men recovering the vehicle with a winch, and others had been tramping all over the spot, obscuring and destroying any forensic evidence there might have been. The first policeman on the scene had removed a small leather holdall from the back seat of the car, where it was lying next to a flat tyre. (It seemed that somewhere en route from Glasgow on the evening of 5th April, McRae had stopped, changed the flat for a brand new tyre, stuck it on the back seat and continued on his way.) He asked David Coutts to put McRae's belongings into this holdall. This of course would not have been allowed had it been known at the time that the victim had been shot.

While gathering up what possessions he could find, Coutts found a pile of torn-up papers about 15 yards from the car, which included a credit-card bill, a garage invoice and, oddly, the face from McRae's watch. There were also some books and a Bible, and a half-bottle of whisky was found in the glove compartment. But there was no briefcase, no other documents or papers, which he would normally have taken with him to his cottage to work on over the weekend. Indeed, neighbours in Glasgow who had seen him leave at 6.30 the previous evening remembered seeing him with briefcase, papers and notes for a book he was writing on the nuclear industry. None of these was ever to be seen again.

Nor was there any sign of the Gold Flake cigarettes that McRae chain-smoked: he would normally have carried several packets but there were none in the car. There was, however, a possible explanation for this: on the Thursday night, in his home in the South Side of Glasgow after spending the evening at a friend's, he had been smoking in bed and fallen asleep. He woke in the early hours to find the bed on fire. He jumped up, carried the burning sheets and blankets to his bathroom and dumped them in the sink, turning on the taps. But the bathroom suite was new, and made of acrylic, and it too caught fire. Thick smoke soon overcame him. Fortunately two men passing by saw the smoke coming from a window and called the fire brigade. Before they arrived, the men had broken into the flat and found McRae lying on the floor, semi-conscious. They rescued him and the fire was extinguished. It is argued that after this narrow escape McRae decided to give up smoking completely and threw away all his cigarettes.

The unknown factor in this incident was whether McRae was drunk when he went to bed. He certainly liked a drink, and some thought he drank too heavily. Then there was the whisky bottle in the glove compartment. Had he been drinking on the road from Glasgow to Dornie that night? He had already had one drink-driving conviction, and was due to appear in court on a second charge. If he lost control of the wheel that night and crashed, might his remorse and shame have driven him to suicide? He did possess a .22 revolver, and indeed when the police returned to the scene the gun was found in the burn. It had been fired twice. The official version of events seemed to be that, having crashed the car, McRae, who was suffering stress and emotional problems, took his own life, firing the gun once to test it, then placing it to his head and pulling the trigger a second time.

A whole raft of objections can be raised against this explanation. How did the gun come to be in the burn, some distance from the 'suicide' victim? Accounts vary as to how far away it was—from twenty feet to twenty yards—but it was too far to have fallen from McRae's hand after he shot himself. He might have thrown it through the window, but the idea of a fatally wounded man bothering to fling away the gun in such a way seems odd. Given the position of the car, it seems remarkable that the weapon ended up in the water, and under an overhang of grass and heather. In any event, medical opinion was that, although he survived, presumably through the night, the wound to the brain was so severe that any motor functions would have been instantly curtailed, making the act of throwing the gun away highly improbable.

It has also been established that blood-tests for alcohol taken on the body proved negative. Tiredness or inattention remain possibilities, but McRae knew the road extremely well, and the corner where the car was found is not an especially tricky one. In any event, that would hardly explain why he was killed by a bullet.

Was McRae suicidal? None of his friends seemed to think so. In fact, he had been in high spirits over the prospects for his book on the nuclear industry, having apparently found some damning or potentially explosive evidence against those he considered his enemies. 'I've got them! I've got them!' he had said gleefully, but did not elaborate. He had also put his name forward as an objector in the forthcoming public inquiry into establishing a nuclear waste reprocessing plant at Dounreay. Ironically, this inquiry would open exactly a year after his death.

He was a bachelor. Some have suggested he was homosexual and that this in some way contributed to his decision to take his life. Again, family and friends deny that he was homosexual, but even if he was this seems an implausible reason for a 61-year-old man to take his life in the 1980s. Business worries, his connections with extreme nationalist organisations, his drinking, all have been suggested as possible reasons for suicide. But against these is the evidence of many that he was in cheerful spirits in the days leading up to his death. His diary was full of appointments for the following week. He had met a client on the Thursday, coming out of a Glasgow bookshop clutching several new books he intended to read. He had, perhaps, given up smoking. This is not the behaviour of a man planning to kill himself. Nor does a man decide to kill himself on the spur of a moment, after a car accident which he has survived unharmed, at the side of a deserted Highland road. Too much does not add up.

If he had not given up smoking, where were his missing cigarettes? Where were his papers? Where was the £100-pound note—his first legal fee—which he carried with him at all times as a lucky charm. What were the torn-up documents doing near the car? Had he got out via the passenger door, disposed of them and these other items (they were never found at or near the scene), got back in his car, moved into the driver's seat, wound down the window, fired the gun once, then shot himself? The scenario is too bizarre. Only his fingerprints were found on the gun, but the wound (not, apparently discovered until he was transferred to Aberdeen) had no traces of the burns and soot which are characteristic of a contact-wound (i.e. one where the barrel is placed up against the skin). Similarly, there was none of the usual forensic evidence to suggest that the gun had been fired, say, two or three inches away from the temple. The wound in fact bore closest resemblance to a longer-range shot, but the position of the car meant that such a shot could not have entered the head from the side. What then of the shattered rear window? Could a bullet have been fired from behind? Could the temple wound have been an exit wound? Apparently not, since the official report states that the bullet was found in the brain. How then did the rear window come to be shattered, when the Volvo had sustained very little other damage?

Was McRae murdered? If so, by whom? Somebody who knew McRae's movements, knew that he would go from Glasgow to his cottage that night, knew that the road around nine o'clock would be virtually traffic-free? Somebody who removed vital evidence from the scene of the crime before anyone else arrived? If so, why did they use McRae's own gun? Why did they throw it away, when they must have realised it would be found later? The possibility exists that another .22 revolver was used, that McRae's gun was fired twice and left as a plant, to indicate suicide.

Who would have killed him? The obvious suspects are the British security services. McRae was an unlikely individual to be considered a real danger to the state, but he had made it his business to ferret out information on nuclear power, and might just have secured some knowledge that was considered too vital to be allowed into the public domain. McRae's cottage had apparently been broken into more than once, and his Glasgow home once in 1984. Nothing had been taken—perhaps because whatever was being looked for was not found?

The official reaction to the death was a massive exercise in stonewalling. There was a growing clamour for a full inquiry. The initial response of Thomas Aitchison, procurator fiscal at Inverness, was that there were *no suspicious circumstances*! He modified this view after pressure from various sources, and as new information came to light. But in early July 1985, some three months after the incident, the Crown Office announced that there would be no inquiry, and that the Crown was satisfied as to the events surrounding Mr McRae's death. In part, this was due to the wishes of the dead man's family, as represented by his brother Dr Fergus McRae. The Crown concluded that 'no further information on the circumstances of this death will be made public.' Peter Fraser, the Solicitor General, now Lord Fraser of Carmyllie, stated: 'I personally took the decision that there should be no fatal accident inquiry. This is not unusual where the circumstances, so far as ascertained, reveal no criminality on the part of another person known or unknown.' This seemed at the time, and seems now, an astonishing conclusion to have reached.

Within the SNP, suspicions would not be allayed. It launched its own investigation, headed by Winnie Ewing, the European MP for the Highlands and Islands and herself a lawyer. Ewing made a long study, asking for input from various friends and acquaintances of the deceased, including Michael Strathern, who had been expelled from the SNP for membership of Siol nan Gaidheal and who knew more about McRae's alleged clandestine activities than anyone. Strathern, among others, was convinced that, whatever happened to his old friend, he had not killed himself. After two years, Ewing asked for all the relevant papers submitted by the procurator fiscal's office. She undertook, as a lawyer, that she would treat these confidentially: if, having analysed them, she was satisfied that the cause of death was indeed suicide, the matter would be dropped by the SNP. As it turned out, she need not have bothered with this pre-emptive attempt at calming negotiations. The Crown Office refused to release the material.

Since then the SNP has allowed the matter to rest. Winnie Ewing has made no further comment on the case. Gordon Wilson, the then party leader, pointed out that the wishes of the family should be respected, and that he himself had always considered that McRae had committed suicide. It is likely that the SNP, as it began to recover its electoral popularity in the second half of the 1980s, found the whole affair awkward, and McRae's enthusiasms and contacts potentially embarrassing politically. There have been several books written since then in which all the inconsistencies and unanswered questions surrounding the events of that night in April 1985 are raised. But without the co-operation of officialdom, the mystery of Willie McRae's death will probably not be solved. Nor, by the same token, can many people resist the notion that something very strange happened by Loch Loyne, and that Willie McRae did not die by his own hand. The Willie McRae Society was formed, with Michael Strathern among its number, and it erected a cairn near the spot where McRae died, dedicated to the memory of 'a Scottish patriot'. 'The struggle goes on', it reads. Every year, a few people gather to remember him. And to question once again, why and how it was that he died.

FILE NO: 032
SUBJECT: .... ritual sacrifice
LOCATION: .... nr. Balloch, Loch Lomond
DATE: .... August 1983
CLASSIFICATION: .... n/a
STATUS: .... closed

IN THE FOOTSTEPS OF CROWLEY

The trial for murder, in January 1986, of Sheena McLaughlan and Alan Porter, must rank as one of the most bizarre in recent Scottish legal history. They were accused of murdering Sheena's three-month-old baby Kether, two and a half years before, and disposing of the body somewhere in the vicinity of Loch Lomond.

Sheena McLaughlan was a bright and promising Glasgow girl, born in 1961, who from an early age developed an interest in the occult, especially in the use of tarot cards. She was educated at Woodside Secondary, and later went to Napier College in Edinburgh, but failed to qualify there, as she became increasingly interested in various aspects of occultism. In 1982 she went to London, and, when she returned to her mother's home in Maryhill at the end of that year, she was pregnant. The identity of the father was not known. McLaughlan said she was pregnant by 'immaculate conception': she had had an unworldly experience on Salisbury Plain, near the Stonehenge stone circle.

The child, a girl, was born on 9th May 1983, and McLaughlan called her Kether Boleskine. Kether is the name of one of the points on the Qabalistic tree of life. Boleskine derives from the name of the house beside Foyers on Loch Ness which was owned in the first half of this century by Aleister Crowley, the self-styled 'wickedest man in the world' [*See File No. 027*]. Crowley's promotion of the black arts had made its mark on McLaughlan, as on many other impressionable occultists.

Around the time of the birth McLaughlan met Alan Porter, a painter and decorator with claims to being a spiritualist. McLaughlan told Porter that she feared her mother would take Kether away from her. That summer, her mother went on holiday to Florida. It was the last she ever saw of her granddaughter.

On 26th August, McLaughlan and Porter set off from Maryhill, pushing Kether in a pram, walking 25 miles to Balloch on the shore of Loch Lomond. At a deserted spot somewhere near the loch, the life of the baby came to a sudden and violent end.

Later, McLaughlan would say that Kether had gone to her father in England. She lied to her mother that the baby was fine and well. By the time her mother returned from holiday,

McLaughlan and Porter had gone to Brighton and were staying with friends of his. But Sheena McLaughlan was clearly in an unhealthy state of mind, knowing that she had committed a terrible act. With Porter she journeyed north again, to friends in North Uist, but they did not stay there long. Soon they were back in Glasgow, living in Porter's flat in the Gorbals, but shortly afterwards they split up.

For a while McLaughlan took up with an acquaintance of Porter's, William Borland, and moved into his caravan at Errogie in the Highlands—just a mile or two from Boleskine House. It was to Borland that she first confessed that Kether had been murdered at Loch Lomond. In May 1984, when the baby would have been having her first birthday, they returned to Loch Lomond, where McLaughlan left Borland on his own while she went in search of the grave where Kether lay buried. But she could not find the body, only one or two items such as the baby's hairbrush. Hysterical with grief, she told Borland that Porter had killed her baby.

Borland got out of the relationship soon after this. In August McLaughlan contacted her mother again, claiming that Kether had died of cancer. But she was clearly distressed and in deep emotional trouble. Eventually she broke down and told her mother that Porter had killed Kether and they had buried her at the loch.

The police were called in. McLaughlan was now being treated at Stobhill Hospital for acute psychiatric disorders. It was some time before she could give her story to the police. When she did, it was both shocking and bizarre.

Porter, she said, had made her push the pram all the way to Loch Lomondside. He had drugged her in some way, she claimed, and was angry because the baby would not stop crying. At the loch, Porter took the baby and McLaughlan went away for a walk. When she came back Porter told her that Kether was dead.

McLaughlan also told the police that after the birth she had had visions of her spiritual guide, a Tibetan monk, who appeared in his saffron robes and told her that her child must die. 'I kept getting these premonitions,' she said. 'I kept seeing my baby's head covered in blood.'

McLaughlan took police to the scene of the crime. A new search was made. A bottle was found, and items of baby clothing, but no corpse. Park rangers remembered finding a pram near the spot, which was handed over to the police at Alexandria and later disposed of as an unclaimed item. It was never traced. Meanwhile the hunt was on for Alan Porter. He was finally traced, via Glasgow and Aberdeen, to Hove near Brighton. When he was interviewed, he confessed to the murder. However, he implicated McLaughlan, saying that she had tried to choke the baby, and that he, 'to put it out of its suffering', had taken it from her and finished the job, strangling Kether with his bare hands. He buried the body wrapped in a pink blanket. He claimed that, after it was over, McLaughlan wanted to have sex there in the woods, but that he had refused.

Each thus blamed the other. Each claimed that the other had been the instigator—the one who wanted rid of the baby dominating the other by sheer force of will. Porter told a doctor who visited him in Barlinnie Prison that Sheena had insisted: 'the baby has to die'. He was under her control, as she exerted a great spiritual power over him. She, on the other hand, said that Alan had manipulated and drugged her. On the night of the murder, the couple had walked from Loch Lomond to Drymen, where they had gone to the local police station and McLaughlan had told a story that her bag had been stolen and that they had no money to get back to Glasgow. The police officer on duty recalled that McLaughlan was confident and articulate, while Porter was downcast and quiet.

In the end, when brought to trial, McLaughlan changed her plea and was found guilty of culpable homicide, while Porter was found guilty of murder. The difference reflected McLaughlan's desperate psychological condition at the time of the trial. This convinced the judge and jury that she was not responsible for her actions, although she remained culpable for handing over Kether to Porter when it was clear he intended to harm her. McLaughlan was given a five-year sentence. Porter got life.

The baby's corpse has never been found. After two years, anything could have happened: wild animals might have uncovered it, or it might have been destroyed by winter snows, floods and inevitable decomposition. But a body need not be found to prove a charge of murder. Kether Boleskine was, it seems, the innocent victim of a bizarre murder, motivated by a mixture of self-interest and ritualistic sacrifice.

FILE NO: 033
SUBJECT: .... Ben Alder corpse
LOCATION: ....Ben Alder, Inverness-shire
DATE: .... June 1996 to November 1997
CLASSIFICATION: .... n/a
STATUS: .... closed

THE MAN WITH NO NAME

Two Glasgow hillwalkers out in the mountains of Inverness-shire had a nasty shock in June 1996. They found a body, but it was not that of another hillwalker who had slipped and been killed in a climbing accident. The man they found had died of a gunshot wound to the chest.

Three weeks after the discovery, the Northern Constabulary had made no progress in establishing who the man was or how he had come to die on the upper slopes of Ben Alder, a wild and challenging 3,774-foot mountain near Dalwhinnie. They issued a description of the man in an attempt to solve the mystery, stressing that there were no suspicious circumstances. It appeared that the man had killed himself, and that his body had lain under snow and ice, perhaps for several months, before being spotted after the spring thaw.

Police described him as being between 45 and 55, 5 feet 6 inches tall, of slim build and with medium-short brown hair. He had no distinguishing surgical scars and there was no evidence of heart disease. He was wearing a green three-quarter length waterproof jacket, French black denim jeans, two vests, a short-sleeved white shirt and a crewneck oatmeal wool jumper. But his footwear was decidedly unsuitable for walking in the hills, especially in winter. He was wearing fashionable brown leather designer shoes with brass buckles, made in Italy by Sopran. His wristwatch was a French Inotime quartz model. Also found was a new green and purple Karrimor rucksack, containing a French-made sleeping-bag and three water containers. The gun found near him was a replica of an 1858 Remington army revolver, a close cousin of the famous Colt range, the long-barrelled handguns made famous by their role in the Wild West. This model fires six balls and requires a separate input of gunpowder. A gunpowder flask, kept dry inside a cigar box, was also recovered on the mountain.

At first it was hoped that these facts about the weapon might be the start of a trail leading to the man's identity, as it was not reckoned to be a common model. Chief Inspector Alasdair Sutherland was quoted as saying that one of the reasons for the public appeal was to find out where someone would get such a gun. 'We are considering the possibility that it may not have been held on a firearms certificate.' It transpired, however, that such replicas, made in Italy, are easily purchased over the counter in French supermarkets.

The body was found propped up against a cairn, overlooking a spectacular view. Rocks had prevented the body from slipping over into a 1,000-foot drop. It did seem likely that the unknown man had chosen the lonely spot for a purpose, and that that purpose was suicide.

But there were unanswered questions. A post-mortem confirmed that he had died from the chest wound, and that this had been caused by a shot from the gun. The gun was found near his left hand. If he used this hand, it appeared that he had shot himself with the gun turned towards his chest, pulling the trigger with his thumb. It was certainly not a way guaranteed to cause death, let alone a quick and easy death.

Then there was the fact that no-one had reported anybody answering his description as missing. When a blank was drawn in the UK, Interpol were called in, and the search was extended to France and Italy. The body's fingerprints were taken and a description of his teeth, dental work etc. passed on to Interpol. The dead man had been at pains to hide his identity: he had no personal papers or belongings on him giving a clue as to who he was, and all but one of the labels had been cut off his clothing. A railway timetable for the Glasgow to Fort William route was in the rucksack, as was a map of the area, and in one pocket was £21. Some food and toiletries (British-bought) were also found. Detective Sergeant Calum Macrae in Aviemore was quoted as saying: 'This case is most bizarre and intriguing. We cannot absolutely rule out foul play . . . but it is unlikely, given the location he was found. However, we don't know what can of worms may be opened once we discover his identity.'

That was in October 1996. Three months later, the police were no nearer a solution. They decided on a new and highly unusual plan—to reconstruct what the man's face might have looked like using computer graphics. Having lain unfound for as long as six months, some decomposition had occurred, but from photographs of the head, Di Cullington, an expert in craniofacial identification, and a world-renowned figure in the field of computer age progression, composite drawing and skull reconstruction techniques, was able to build up an image of the man's features. This reconstruction was then circulated throughout Europe. As Detective Sergeant Macrae said: 'Maybe somebody will know who he was.'

The continued silence from friends or relatives of the missing person—by now the case had had considerable public exposure—was odd. Could the man have had no family or personal connections? And why, especially if he was from a foreign country, had he come to Ben Alder to die? Had he been there before? It appeared he had boarded the Fort William train at Glasgow, and got off at Corrour, the popular halt for hillwalkers in the middle of Rannoch Moor. Nobody at Corrour, apparently, noticed anything unusual about a single man (assuming he was alone) who seemed well-equipped for the rough terrain—apart, that is, from his footwear. From the station, it is about an 18-mile walk across the moor, through the Ben Alder estate and on to the mountain. He may have stopped overnight at Ben Alder cottage, an isolated bothy, but nobody could be traced who remembered sharing the place with such a man. Climbing almost to the summit of Ben Alder, the man left the main track and, presumably, shot himself.

He may have taken his own life in this lonely place for any number of reasons. Did he choose the grandeur of the mountain scenery as a fitting place to end his life? Did he not want to be found for some time after his death? Or did someone else not want him to be found? The possibility remains that he was not alone on his walk to the mountain. That someone else pulled the trigger and left the gun by his hand to make it look like suicide. A murderer, it would seem, would have far greater reason for removing all marks of identity than a man going out to end his own life.

It seemed likely that, until the enigma of his identity was resolved, speculation about why he died would continue. Then, in November 1997, the breakthrough came. Following a contact made with a French family in August 1997, genetic fingerprinting and forensic odontology evidence finally revealed the identity of the Ben Alder man. As the police had long suspected, he was indeed a Frenchman. His name was Emmanuel Caillet, a 26-year-old who had gone missing from his home near Paris in August 1995. He had arrived in Scotland in the autumn of that year. Exactly why and how he met his death on Ben Alder may never be known, but at least, as Detective Sergeant Macrae stated in a Northern Constabulary Press Release issued on 6th November 1997, the case had been brought 'to a successful if tragic conclusion'.

McX
034

FILE NO: 034
SUBJECT: .... miniature coffins
LOCATION: .... Arthur's Seat, Edinburgh
DATE: .... June 1836
CLASSIFICATION: .... n/a
STATUS: .... open

THE SEVENTEEN COFFINS OF BURKE AND HARE

On Saturday 25th June 1836, five schoolboys set off for Arthur's Seat, the 823-foot hill which dominates Holyrood Park in Edinburgh. They took with them two dogs, and a couple of trowels, as their intention was to go rabbiting on the north-eastern slopes of the hill.

Late in the morning, they came across a curious entrance in the hill, which one of the dogs was sniffing around, presumably thinking it a rabbit burrow. As *The Scotsman* newspaper reported three weeks later, this 'small opening in one of the rocks' was in 'a very rugged and secluded spot'. 'The mouth of this little cave,' the paper said, 'was closed by three thin pieces of slatestone, rudely cut at the upper end into a conical form, and so placed as to protect the interior from the effects of the weather.' The boys removed these slates, and discovered a space about twelve inches square, inside which were placed seventeen tiny coffins, carefully arranged in three tiers, two of eight coffins and the third, the topmost, having only one coffin, as if it were a layer only recently begun. 'The coffins,' said *The Scotsman*, 'are about three or four inches in length, and cut out from a single piece of wood, with the exception of the lids, which are nailed down with wire sprigs or common brass pins. The lid and sides of each are profusely studded with ornaments formed of small pieces of tin, and inserted in the wood with great care and regularity.'

The boys, apparently, made no attempt to open these tiny boxes, a fact which is hard to believe. They did, however, take them out and toss them around in play, damaging and indeed destroying a few; but, perhaps sensing that there was something odd about their discovery, they replaced the others as found, and later told their schoolmaster, a Mr Ferguson, about their adventure.

Ferguson was a keen amateur archaeologist, and he asked the boys to show him the spot. The coffins were there just as they had described them. Ferguson removed them and took them home for examination. When he prised off the lids of these strange artefacts, he discovered that each contained a wooden figure, again carved in wood, lying like a corpse within. The faces of these figures seemed to have been delicately and carefully carved so that the human features were quite clearly delineated. Each 'body' was dressed in cotton funeral clothes, and had black painted boots; some of the coffins had been lined with cloth. It looked as though great care, even reverence, had been taken to 'lay out' the bodies.

It was also clear that the coffins had not been placed in their tomb all at the same time. Some showed greater signs of decay than others. The newspaper reported, 'many years must have elapsed since the first interment took place in this mysterious sepulchre, and it is also evident that the depositions must have been made singly and at considerable intervals—facts indicated by the rotten and decayed state of the first tier of coffins and their wooden mummies and the wrapping cloths being in some instances entirely mouldered away.' The single coffin in the third tier, on the other hand, was as clean and fresh as if it had been put there only days before.

The Scotsman could not find any satisfactory explanation for what it called this 'singular fantasy of the human mind', a phenomenon which seemed 'rather above insanity, and yet much beneath rationality'. The newspaper's own opinion would be, it concluded, 'had we not some years ago abjured witchcraft and demonology', that there were still a few witches who gathered on the hill, who retained 'their ancient power to work these spells of death by entombing the likenesses of those they wish to destroy'. If this were the case, the boys were to be congratulated on discovering and destroying 'this satanic spell-manufactory, the last we should hope that the "infernal hags" will ever be permitted to erect in Scotland!'

That might have been the end of the matter, but considerable speculation was aroused over the discovery. *The Times* ran half a column on the story. One view suggested that the relics might date back hundreds of years. This was soon dismissed, as the white cotton in which the figures were dressed was found to date only from the 1820s or early 1830s. The coffins were displayed in the private museum of a jeweller, Mr Frazer, of South St Andrew Street, and were seen by many people.

It is not entirely clear what became of the figures for some decades after this. However, in March 1902, eight of the coffins and their contents reappeared when they were presented to the National Museum of Antiquities by a Mrs Couper, of Tymon Manse, Dumfries. It is not known how they came into her possession, but they remain in the care of the National Museum of Scotland to this day. Along with them, the Museum acquired a letter, apparently throwing some light on the subject. According to this letter, written by a woman resident in Edinburgh in 1836, around the time of the coffins' discovery her father's office was frequently visited by a deaf and dumb man who was also 'daft'. Not long after the removal of the coffins from Arthur's Seat, this man turned up in the office in a state of great agitation, clutching a sheet of paper, on which was a sketch of three coffins, bearing the dates 1837, 1839 and 1840. This was the last time the man appeared in the office, and he was never heard of again. By coincidence, however, the woman's father died in 1837, and two other relatives died in 1839 and 1840. The woman's theory was that this strange person, who for some reason had an obsession with burial, had been responsible for making the seventeen coffins and corpses, and that their removal had deeply distressed and upset him. But nothing more ever came to light about him.

In November 1993, the Museum in Chambers Street put the surviving eight coffins back on display. And now, a plausible explanation for them was offered, by Dr Sam Menefee, an American lawyer and anthropologist based at the University of Virginia. He suggested that there was a connection between the seventeen 'corpses' and the victims of the notorious murderers Burke and Hare. William Burke and William Hare, two Irishmen who ran lodgings for the poor in Edinburgh's West Port, sold the bodies of their victims for medical research, notably to the anatomist Robert Knox, who received the bodies on a 'no questions asked' basis. It is thought that the first body, that of an elderly man who died in their lodgings, was sold in order to make up for rent that he owed. Having got a taste for easy money, the two men subsequently finished off lodgers, down-and-outs and others by suffocation. They were not, as is commonly believed, 'resurrectionists' or bodysnatchers.

Dr Menefee's theory has a certain attraction: the murders were carried out over a period in the late 1820s, thus tying in with the dating attached to the miniature coffins. Tests carried out at the Museum revealed that the figures in the coffins were not carved as corpses, as previously thought, but were in fact toy soldiers dating from the late 18th century. The possibility that they were effigies used in some witchcraft ceremony was also ruled out—contrary to earlier stories, they had not been stuck with pins. Possibly someone with knowledge of the crimes placed the corpses on Arthur's Seat as a kind of atonement, or as a memorial to each victim. Or perhaps they were placed later, after William Burke's trial and execution in 1829 (Hare turned king's evidence and survived, to the fury of the Edinburgh population) by an intrigued or morbid member of the public, who symbolically buried them so that the souls of the murder victims might rest in peace. Could the deaf and dumb man be somehow connected?

Against the theory, Burke and Hare are generally reckoned to have murdered only sixteen people, although there will always be doubt as to the exact number. But the seventeenth coffin, set alone on its tier, might relate either to the old man who was not murdered but whose body was sold, or it might even relate to the hanged William Burke himself. In the absence of any other explanation, a connection with the Burke and Hare murders certainly seems highly plausible, although it is unlikely now that any final solution to the mystery will be found.

FILE NO: 035
SUBJECT: .... death of Norah Fornario
LOCATION: ....Isle of Iona
DATE: ....November 1929
CLASSIFICATION: AN5
STATUS: .... open

THE ORDER OF ALPHA AND OMEGA

In the Reilig Odhráin burial ground on Iona, the holy island settled by Columba as a place of learning and worship in the 6th century AD, lie the graves of numerous ancient Scottish kings. More recently the body of John Smith, the leader of the Labour Party until his death in 1994, was laid to rest there. But there is another unusual gravestone in Reilig Odhráin, which bears only the message: 'N.E.F. died 19 November 1929. Aged 33 years.'

This is the grave of Norah Emily Fornario, who travelled to Iona in that year of 1929, a journey that was considerably more arduous then than it is now. The long road across Mull to Fionnphort was then a track, and in late autumn the conditions were far from good. But Norah Fornario was on a quest, which brought her to the sanctity and special atmosphere of Iona, that place of which Dr Johnson wrote: 'That man is little to be envied . . . whose piety would not grow warmer among the ruins of Iona.'

The Church of Scotland had restored the ruined abbey in the early years of the century, and there was a small but settled crofting community on the island when Fornario arrived. She stayed at the Cameron croft at Traighmòr, and was, though something of a novelty to the islanders, left to her own devices. She had come on a spiritual journey as much as a physical one, and spent her days wandering the small island, crossing the moorland and visiting the white-sanded beaches, reading and writing poetry and contemplating the occult matters with which she was obsessed.

For Fornario was interested in spirit communication and spiritualism—as were many in her day. Indeed the 1920s saw a huge increase in interest in these subjects: Arthur Conan Doyle was a foremost figure in spiritualist circles. But Fornario was perhaps more naive than some of those she became involved with. Among her mentors were Samuel Liddell Mathers and his wife Mina. Samuel was a magician who brought much of the Qabalist and esoteric tradition of continental Europe to Britain. Mina was a well-known clairvoyant and medium. They encouraged Fornario's interest in faith-healing, tarot and telepathy, and she became a member of the Order of Alpha and Omega, an offshoot of the Mathers' Hermetic Order of the Golden Dawn.

The Mathers were, in today's terms, what one might

call 'control freaks'. The Order of the Golden Dawn was theirs, and they were determined not to lose their grip on how it functioned. Mathers believed that he was descended from the Children of the Mist, the clan MacGregor which had been outlawed and its name proscribed by successive Scottish regimes, and called himself Comte MacGregor of Glenstrae. He maintained a firm command over the lodges of his order in Paris, Bradford, London, Weston-super-Mare and Edinburgh.

He had reckoned, however, without the equally large ego of another magician, who joined the Order in 1898. This was Aleister Crowley [*see File No. 027*], then only 23, but already a forceful and manipulative personality. A battle for control of the Hermetic Order ensued, with both mundane and unearthly forces being employed on both sides. Mathers apparently summoned a vampire to deal with Crowley, who retaliated by unleashing psychic hounds on his opponent. Mathers's magic was too strong, however, and the young 'Beast' was expelled from the Order. He went on, of course, to found his own occult movement.

Three decades after these events, Norah Fornario was involved with the Mathers. She had been only a child when the battle with Crowley had taken place, but the Mathers were still prominent occultists and under their influence she pursued her new age interests. She was in her mid-thirties, her tall dark appearance betrayed her Italian ancestry, and the people of Iona found her pleasant and, although eccentric, unintrusive. What brought her to Iona is not certain, but she was given to going into trances while practising her telepathic faith-healing, to sitting up writing all night, or to going out in the dark and, she claimed, making contact with the many spirits which still roamed the holy island. This behaviour was apparently tolerated remarkably well by local people, for all that they lived in the cradle of Scottish Christianity. When she went missing once, there was no lack of volunteers for a search party. On that occasion, she was found safe and well.

One Sunday late in November, Fornario decided that she must get off the island at once. But, being a Sunday, the ferry to Fionnphort was not running. She packed her bags in readiness for departure the next morning, and, some say in a state of considerable anxiety, took off for another nocturnal walk that evening.

In the morning the Camerons in whose croft she had been staying found her bed unslept in. Her clothes were folded neatly beside it. Some of the crofters set out in search of the missing woman later that day, but with no success. It was not until the following day that Fornario was discovered, not washed up on the shoreline, as had been feared, but in the hills south of Loch Staonaig. She was naked except for the robe of the Order of Alpha and Omega. There was a silver chain around her neck. The soles of her feet were bloody and swollen from having walked, or possibly run, across the rough terrain. Had she been trying to escape from something or somebody? In one hand she held a long knife. When they removed her body from where it lay, it was discovered that a rough cross had been cut out of the turf beneath her.

What killed Norah Emily Fornario? The doctor who completed the death certificate pronounced heart failure. Given the state of her body, and the fact that she died exposed on a cold November night on a Scottish island, this is highly likely. But some have suggested that she died by an unseen hand—by what is known as 'psychic attack'. This would have involved an enemy summoning up some terrible force from the other-world to pursue and terrorise her to death—much as Samuel Mathers and Aleister Crowley had called on vampires, devils and hellhounds in their psychic battles thirty years before. Fornario was a dabbler—she would not have had the skills of these practised magicians to defend herself against such forces. Some have even gone so far as to point the finger at a possible aggressor: Mina Mathers. It is suggested that Fornario may have offended the woman who was once her mentor and who certainly had the knowledge and will, if anyone had, to launch a psychic attack. The look of abject terror found on Fornario's face by the searchers, it is said, was terrible to behold. Possibly, when she looked upon death that night in 1929, it came from beyond the shores of peaceful Iona.

```
FILE NO: .................................... 036
SUBJECT: ....... William T. Linskill, ghost-hunter
LOCATION: ........................ St Andrews/Fife
DATE: ............................c. 1868 to 1888
CLASSIFICATION: .......................... AN3
STATUS: ................................. open
```

'THE WONDERS THAT LIE UNDERGROUND'

The Victorian ghost-hunter and antiquarian, William T. Linskill, was one of Scotland's first, and most dedicated, investigators of paranormal phenomena. A well-known and respected resident of St Andrews in Fife, he collected a great many ghost stories and legends relating to the history of the town, but his abiding ambition was to encounter a ghost himself. This ambition, however, was never fulfilled, as he admitted in 1921: 'It is a sad, nay, a melancholy fact (for I have been told this by the very best authorities) that *I am not psychic*, despite the fact that I have spent days and nights in gloomy, grimly-haunted chambers and ruins, and even a lonesome Hallowe'en night on the summit of St Rule's ancient tower (my only companions being sandwiches, matches, some cigars, and the necessary and indispensable flask), yet, alas! I have *never* heard or seen anything the least abnormal, or felt the necessary, or much talked of, mystic presence.'

Yet this personal disappointment did not dampen Linskill's enthusiasm for all things paranormal, and one particular mystery became a lifelong obsession—the search for 'Underground St Andrews'. After visiting the Catacombs in Rome, Linskill became convinced, despite a singular lack of evidence, that a similar complex of underground passages and chambers existed beneath St Andrews, connecting the ancient castle with the cathedral and the surrounding ecclesiastical buildings.

Towards the end of the 1870s, Linskill was staying with friends in Edinburgh when he met a Mr Ashton, who told him a very curious tale of an encounter on the Fife coast. Ashton had been staying near St Andrews in one of the small coastal towns of the East Neuk of Fife—most probably Crail or Pittenweem. One evening, as he walked alone on the beach, he met a strange old man who showed him a cave or cleft in the rocks along the shoreline. Following the old man into the cave, Ashton found himself at the foot of a staircase which ascended, via some thirty or so steps, into the cliffs, and appeared to have been hewn from the solid rock. At the top of the steps was a narrow passage which the old man informed him had been used by the monks of a nearby monastery that had long since disappeared. Ashton went on to describe all manner of terrifying sights and experiences in the darkness of the tunnels and chambers the old man led him through—at one point he even claimed to have heard the tolling of bells, which the old man said were ghostly echoes of the bells of the ruined Cathedral of St Andrews. After they had covered a considerable distance underground, Ashton suddenly lost sight of his companion and found himself completely alone in the darkness. Confused and by now very frightened, he stumbled and fell down a flight of stone steps and lost consciousness. When he regained his senses, Ashton was astonished to find himself above ground once more, just inside the old gateway to the Pends—part of the medieval walls that surround St Andrews Cathedral.

Clearly, this story fitted in with Linskill's ideas about 'underground St Andrews', and he set about finding the entrance to the cave Ashton had described. He found the place easily enough, but the cave had fallen in and obliterated any trace of the staircase Ashton claimed to have ascended. Similarly, Linskill was unable to find any evidence of the exit from which Ashton had emerged in the Pends.

Then, in 1879, a startling discovery close to the castle walls seemed to back up Ashton's story. During the demolition of the old Keeper's cottage adjacent to the castle, an extensive and previously unknown subterranean passage was uncovered. Linskill's hopes were soon dashed, however, when it was revealed that this was not the entrance to the lost passages of 'underground St Andrews'—it turned out to be the remains of a mine and counter-mine, dating from the siege of the Castle of 1546-7.

As ever, Linskill was not dispirited and his quest for the secret passages continued. Although deeply sceptical about spiritualism, he attended a séance, held in a house in South Street, St Andrews, as part of his search. After a certain amount of what Linskill later referred to as 'tomfoolery' and various 'conjuring tricks', featuring the appearance of a 'spirit arm', a Ouija board was produced by the two mediums who were conducting the séance. Contact was apparently made with a monk named Rudolph, who described a secret chapel or crypt beneath the ruins of the cathedral. The spirit went on to tell Linskill and his companions that this underground chapel was supported by marble pillars and contained three altars—and 'something so horrible it turned him sick. . . .' Despite his profound interest in anything that could shed light on his obsession, Linskill dismissed what he had heard as the complete fabrication of a pair of obvious charlatans. This was to be as close as Linskill got to the secret he believed lay hidden beneath the town. No other significant discoveries were ever made, despite his best efforts and his relentless exploration of St Andrews' many ancient buildings and ruins.

Of the many other investigations Linskill undertook—including a phantom coach, various spectral monks and the screaming skull of Neville de Beauchamp—perhaps the strangest case he investigated was that of the White Lady and the Haunted Tower. Situated within the medieval walls of the cathedral, one of the thirteen fortified towers that originally guarded the precincts of the cathedral had long been reputed to be haunted. The ghostly figure of a 'White Lady' was said to roam the walls in the vicinity and many locals claimed to have seen her—indeed, Ashton claimed to have seen a similar apparition during his underground experience. Linskill set out to uncover the story behind this haunting, and his enquiries soon led him to make a strange discovery. For many years, the two-storey rectangular tower had remained sealed, its evil reputation dissuading those who may have been curious about whatever secrets it contained. Then, in 1868, a group of antiquarians had broken into the tower. This is the account Linskill was given by Jesse Hall, one of those present:

'Mr Smith, watchmaker, and Mr Walker, the University Librarian, who were both antiquaries, pressed me frequently to allow them to open the vault. I did not care about it, as I did not like to disturb the dead; but I at last consented, and early one summer morning before six o'clock—as we did not want to make it public—the three of us, Mr Smith, Mr Walker and myself, went to the place and made a small hole, just enough to admit a man's head and shoulders. The doorway opened into a passage, and round the corner to the left was the vault proper. We all scrambled in, and by the light of a candle which we carried, we saw two chests lying side by side. I cannot say how many chests there were. There would be half a dozen as far as I can remember. I saw the body of a girl. The body was stiff and mummified-like. What appeared to be a glove was on one of the hands. . . . After we went in the first time we shut up the hole and kept the matter a profound secret, and I did not know that anyone knew of it except ourselves. People had been in the habit of calling the place the Haunted Tower and when going to the harbour they ran past it. No-one had any idea that it was a place of burial till we opened it.'

Although he had no idea why this fortified tower had been converted into a tomb, Linskill did put forward several theories as to the possible identity of the 'White Lady', suggesting that what Jesse Hall and his companions had seen could have been the mummified remains of a Celtic saint, a princess, or even a nun who had once been a lady-in-waiting of Mary, Queen of Scots and had retired to a nunnery at St Andrews after a scandalous affair at Court.

Whatever the true identity of the 'White Lady', when Linskill himself reopened the vault in the tower at midnight on the 21st August 1888, he found nothing more than scattered fragments of coffins and a few skeletons. For Linskill, the quest for the truth continued, but the mystery of the 'White Lady', like that of 'the wonders that lie in underground St Andrews', was to remain unsolved. As Linskill himself wrote: 'We may know some day. Or never.'

APPENDIX A

CLASSIFICATION OF PHENOMENA

Two widely-used systems for the classification of unexplained phenomena are detailed below.

The **Hynek System** is named after Dr J. Allen Hynek, a professor of astronomy who took part in a US Air Force investigation into UFOs, code-named *Project Blue Book,* which began in 1952. The project was terminated in 1969, after it was officially discredited. However, many now accept rumours that reports which could not be explained away were mysteriously 'lost'—and that those in authority must therefore not have intended *Blue Book* to succeed.

In 1973, Dr Hynek formed the Center for UFO Studies, the first scientific UFO group. It is from the Hynek System that we get the familiar Close Encounter types.

The Hynek categories are:

Nocturnal Light (NL)—Any anomalous light(s) seen in the night sky whose description rules out the possibilities of aircraft lights, stars, meteors etc.

Daylight Disc (DD)—UFOs seen in the distant sky. May be any shape.

Radar-Visual (RV)—Where UFOs are tracked on radar, and can simultaneously be seen at the corresponding location.

Close Encounters:

Of the First Kind (CEI)—Where a UFO comes close to the witness (within 500 feet).

Of the Second Kind (CEII)—Where the UFO either leaves markings on the ground, causes temporary injury to humans, frightens animals, or interferes with electrical or radio apparatus, etc.

Of the Third Kind (CEIII)—A CEI or CEII in which occupants are visible.

Of the Fourth Kind* (CEIV)—Abduction cases.

Of the Fifth Kind* (CEV)—Communication occurs between a person and an alien.

**Later additions to reflect the growing number of such reports.*

The **Vallée System**, created by Dr Jacques Vallée, a French astrophysicist, is based on Hynek's work, although the list of categories has been greatly expanded in order to be applicable to other areas of paranormal research—Vallée's view is that there may be a psychic dimension to the UFO phenomenon.

The Vallée categories are:

AN (Anomaly) Rating—classifies any anomalous behaviour.

AN1—Anomalies which have no lasting physical effects, e.g. amorphous lights.

AN2—Anomalies which do have lasting physical effects, e.g. where objects are moved or materialised, crop circles.

AN3—Anomalies with associated entities, e.g. ghosts, 'monsters', nature spirits, etc.

AN4—Witness interaction with AN3 entities, e.g. religious or near-death experiences, out-of-body experiences.

AN5—Anomalous events resulting in injury or death, e.g. spontaneous human combustion, unexplained wounding or healing.

MA (Manoeuvre) Rating—describes mobile behaviour of a UFO.

MA1—A UFO which travels in a discontinuous/non-regular trajectory, e.g. sudden changes in speed or height.

MA2—MA1 in which the UFO leaves physical traces of its presence.

MA3—Where entities are observed on board.

MA4—Manoeuvres accompanied by a sense of reality transformation for the witness, e.g. being taken on board.

MA5—A manoeuvre which leads to permanent injury or death.

FB (Fly-By) Rating.

FB1—A simple sighting of a UFO travelling in a straight line across the sky.

FB2—FB1 leaving physical traces.

FB3—Where entities are observed on board.

FB4—A fly-by accompanied by a sense of reality transformation for the witness, e.g. being taken on board.

FB5—A fly-by which leads to permanent injury or death.

CE (Close Encounter) Rating—similar to the Hynek Close Encounter ratings.

CE1—UFO comes within 500 feet of the witness, but with no after-effects or physical traces.

CE2—A CE1 that leaves landing traces or injuries.

CE3—Where entities are observed on board.

CE4—Where the witness is abducted.

CE5—CE4 which leads to permanent psychological/physical injury or death.

SVP (Source/Visit/Possible explanation) Rating—measures the credibility of a report. A score from 0 to 4 is awarded for each of three categories—source reliability, site visit, and possible explanation. The scores are written consecutively, e.g. 201. A rating of 222 or higher is considered good.

Source Reliability Rating.

0—Unknown or unreliable source.

1—Report attributed to a known source of unknown reliability.

2—Reliable source, secondhand.

3—Reliable source, firsthand.

4—Firsthand personal interview with witness and proven reliability of source.

Site Visit Rating.

0—No site visit, or answer unknown.

1—Site visit by a casual observer not familiar with the phenomenon.

2—Site visit by someone familiar with the phenomenon.

3—Site visit by a reliable investigator with some experience.

4—Site visit by a skilled analyst.

Possible Explanation Rating.

0—Data consistent with one or more natural causes.

1—Natural explanation requires only slight modification of the data.

2—Natural explanation requires major alteration of one parameter.

3—Natural explanation requires major alteration of several parameters.

4—No natural explanation possible, given the evidence.

APPENDIX B

FURTHER INFORMATION

Scottish Earth Mysteries Research (SEMR) produces a quarterly magazine, *Phenomenal News*, edited by Viv Alexander. For information about subscriptions, or to submit articles, please write to:

Viv Alexander, 4 Linden Avenue, Stirling, FK7 7PG.

SEMR, in conjunction with Jolly Good Productions, has produced a video called Unknown Scotland (£7.50 including P&P). This is available from:

SEMR, 35 Fountain Road, Bridge of Allan, FK9 4AU.

APPENDIX C

REPORTING AN ENCOUNTER

If you have had a UFO experience, or have video footage or photographic evidence that you would like to report, please write to Ron Halliday at:

SEMR, 35 Fountain Road, Bridge of Allan, FK9 4AU.